Der Froschkönig und andere Kindermärchen

The Frog Prince and other Grimm Fairy Tales

[Bilingual Edition]

German – English

by Jacob and Wilhelm Grimm

Translated by Möwenstein

Contents

Vorwort

Foreword

1.1 Im Gegensatze zu dem kosmopolitischen
Gedankenkreise unserer Klassiker trachtete
zum Beginne des neunzehnten Jahrhunderts die
deutsche sogenannte romantische Schule nach einer
volkstümlichen Nationalpoesie und einer poetisch
verklärten Wiedererweckung der deutschen Vorzeit.

In contrast to the cosmopolitan circle of thought of our
classicists, at the beginning of the nineteenth century the
German so-called Romantic school strove for a popular
national poetry and a poetically transfigured revival of
German prehistory.

1.2 Für die Weiterentwicklung der deutschen Dichtkunst
im allgemeinen ohne belangreiche Wirkung
geblieben, haben diese Bestrebungen, übrigens
einer geschichtlich leicht erklärlichen Reaktion
entsprungen, einer neuen Wissenschaft, der
deutschen Philologie, die Wege geebnet.

While these endeavors had no significant effect on the
further development of German poetry in general, they
paved the way for a new science, German philology, which
was the result of an easily explainable historical reaction.

Ihr eigentlicher Begründer ist Jacob Grimm. 1.3

Its actual founder is Jacob Grimm .

Mit dem Erscheinen seiner »Deutschen Grammatik« 1.4

With the publication of his "German Grammar"

(4 Bände, 1819-1837) hatte die altklassische Philologie 1.5
in der Germanistik eine ebenbürtige Schwester
erhalten.

(4 volumes, 1819-1837), classical philology had found an
equal sister in German studies.

Seine »Deutschen Rechtsalterthümer« (1828, 1834), 1.6
die »Weisthümer«(I-IV, 1840-1863), die »Geschichte
der deutschen Sprache« (1848), die »Deutsche
Mythologie« (1835 u. ö.) und die Inangriffnahme des
»Deutschen Wörterbuches« (1852) boten die reichsten
Anregungen, um tiefer »in die sternenglänzende
Nacht des Mittelalters« einzudringen, barbarische,
bis dahin gehegte Vorurteile zu zerstreuen und eine
objektive Betrachtung vergangener nationaler
Zustände und Eigentümlichkeiten, verbunden
mit der Einsicht in das Gesetz der geschichtlichen
Entwicklung, zu ermöglichen.

His " Deutsche Rechtsalterthümer " (1828, 1834), the
" Weisthümer "(I-IV, 1840-1863), the " Geschichte der
deutschen Sprache " (1848), the " Deutsche Mythologie
" (1835 et al.) and the start of the " German Dictionary
" (1852) offered the richest stimuli to penetrate deeper
"into the starry night of the Middle Ages", to dispel
barbaric, hitherto cherished prejudices and to enable an
objective consideration of past national conditions and
peculiarities, combined with an insight into the law of
historical development.

1.7 Unterstützt in seiner Lebensarbeit wurde Jacob Grimm von seinem gleichgesinnten jüngeren Bruder Wilhelm.

Jacob Grimm was supported in his life's work by his like-minded younger brother Wilhelm.

1.8 Wie die Brüder fast an allen ihren Hauptwerken gemeinsam arbeiteten, so hat sich die dankbare Nachwelt auch daran gewöhnt, überhaupt nur von den »Gebrüdern Grimm« zu reden.

Just as the brothers worked together on almost all of their major works, grateful posterity has also become accustomed to speaking only of the "Brothers Grimm".

2.1 Jacob Ludwig Karl Grimm wurde am 4. Januar 1785 zu Hanau geboren.

Jacob Ludwig Karl Grimm was born in Hanau on January 4, 1785.

2.2 Nachdem er in Marburg studiert (1802 bis 1805) und auf Veranlassung des berühmten deutschen Juristen Savigny acht Monate in Paris verweilt hatte, wurde ihm durch Vermittlung Johannes von Müllers, des bekannten Geschichtschreibers, die Leitung der Privatbibliothek des Königs Jerôme von Westfalen in Wilhelmshöhe übertragen.

After studying in Marburg (1802 to 1805) and spending eight months in Paris at the instigation of the famous German jurist Savigny, he was put in charge of the private library of King Jerôme of Westphalia in Wilhelmshöhe through the mediation of Johannes von Müller, the famous historian.

Sieben Jahre lang konnte er sich hier, während 2.3
Deutschland unter dem Joche der französischen
Fremdherrschaft seufzte, seinen germanistischen
Studien widmen.

For seven years he was able to devote himself to his
Germanic studies here, while Germany groaned under
the yoke of French foreign rule.

Nach der endgiltigen Niederwerfung des 2.4
Korsen und Wiederherstellung der deutschen
Bundesstaatsregierungen wurde er (1816) zweiter
Bibliothekar an der Bibliothek in Kassel, an der
sein Bruder Wilhelm schon seit 1814 als Sekretär
angestellt war.

After the final defeat of Corsica and the restoration of
the German federal state governments, he became (1816)
second librarian at the library in Kassel, where his brother
Wilhelm had been employed as secretary since 1814.

1830 siedelten sie nach Göttingen über, nachdem 2.5
sie mehr als dreizehn Jahre lang vergeblich auf
Beförderung gehofft hatten:

In 1830 they moved to Göttingen after more than thirteen
years of hoping in vain for promotion:

Jacob wurde ordentlicher Professor und 2.6
Bibliothekar,

Jacob became a full professor and librarian,

Wilhelm Unterbibliothekar. 2.7

Wilhelm a junior librarian.

Als aber im Jahre 1837 sieben Göttinger 2.8
Universitätsprofessoren, die berühmten

In 1837, however, when seven Göttingen university
professors, the famous

2.9 »Sieben«, zu denen auch unser Brüderpaar gehörte, gegen den Verfassungsbruch des Königs von Hannover öffentlich Einspruch erhoben, wurden Jacob und Wilhelm Grimm ihres Amtes entsetzt.
"Seven", to which our brothers also belonged, publicly objected to the King of Hanover's breach of the constitution, Jacob and Wilhelm Grimm were removed from office.

2.10 Binnen drei Tagen mußte ersterer das Land verlassen;
Within three days, the former had to leave the country;

2.11 der jüngere Bruder folgte ihm 1838 nach.
the younger brother followed him in 1838.

2.12 Bald nach seiner Thronbesteigung berief indessen König Friedrich Wilhelm IV., der begeisterte Freund des Mittelalters, der
Soon after his accession to the throne, King Frederick William IV. The enthusiastic friend of the Middle Ages, the

2.13 »Romantiker auf dem Throne«, wie ihn ein geistreicher Schriftsteller genannt hat, die beiden als besoldete Akademiker nach Berlin.
"romantic on the throne", as one witty writer called him, appointed them both to Berlin as salaried academics.

2.14 Hier starb Jakob Grimm am 20, September 1863.
Jakob Grimm died here on September 20, 1863.

2.15 Auch an der Nationalerhebung im Sturm - und Drangjahr 1848 hatte er thätigen Anteil genommen, indem er als Vertreter der Stadt Mühlheim nach Frankfurt a. M. ging;
He had also taken an active part in the national uprising of 1848, the year of Sturm und Drang, by going to Frankfurt am Main as a representative of the town of Mühlheim;

doch ist diese Auszeichnung, wie bei Uhland und anderen Dichtern und Gelehrten jener Zeit, mehr als eine in ihrem Idealismus nicht hoch genug zu schätzende Ehrung deutschen Wissens und unbeirrter Wahrheitsliebe von seiten der Wähler aufzufassen. 2.16

however, as with Uhland and other poets and scholars of the time, this distinction should be seen more as a tribute to German knowledge and unwavering love of truth on the part of the voters, the idealism of which cannot be valued highly enough.

Außer den obengenannten Hauptwerken, meist in Gemeinschaft mit Wilhelm Grimm herausgegeben, seien noch genannt: 2.17

In addition to the above-mentioned major works, mostly published in collaboration with Wilhelm Grimm, the following should also be mentioned:

Lieder der alten Edda (1815, mit Wilhelm Grimm), »Deutsche Sagen« (I. 2.18

Lieder der alten Edda (1815, with Wilhelm Grimm), " Deutsche Sagen " (I.

1816, II. 1818, mit Wilhelm Grimm); 2.19

1816, II. 1818, with Wilhelm Grimm);

»Irische Elfenmärchen« (1826 mit Wilhelm Grimm); 2.20

"Irische Elfenmärchen" (1826 with Wilhelm Grimm);

»Reinhart Fuchs« (1834); 2.21

"Reinhart Fuchs " (1834);

»Rede auf Wilhelm Grimm und über das Alter« 2.22

"Rede auf Wilhelm Grimm und über das Alter"

2.23 (1860), welche letztere eine neue Sonderausgabe
verdiente, vielleicht verbunden mit Ciceros
gleichnamigem Werke;
(1860), the latter of which deserved a new special edition,
perhaps combined with Cicero's work of the same name;

2.24 »Kleinere Schriften«
"Kleinere Schriften"

2.25 (I-VII, 1864-1884), die auch eine kurze
Selbstbiographie Jacob Grimms enthalten u. s.
w. Ein vortreffliches Buch über Jacob Grimm hat
Wilhelm Scherer, der verstorbene große Germanist,
veröffentlicht.
(I-VII, 1864-1884), which also contain a short self-biography
of Jacob Grimm, etc. Wilhelm Scherer, the late great
Germanist, published an excellent book on Jacob Grimm.

3.1 Wilhelm Karl Grimm, der jüngere Bruder, am 24,
Februar 1786 zu Hanau geboren, besuchte 1804
ebenfalls die Marburger Hochschule und machte
hier 1806 sein juristisches Examen.
Wilhelm Karl Grimm , the younger brother, born in Hanau
on February 24, 1786, also attended Marburg University in
1804 and passed his law exams there in 1806.

3.2 Während der Herrschaft des Königs Jerôme war er
ohne öffentliche Stellung;
During the reign of King Jerôme he was without a public
position;

3.3 1814 kam er nach Kassel als Bibliothekssekretär.
in 1814 he came to Kassel as library secretary.

Seit 1816 erlebte das Brüderpaar, von gleicher   3.4
Hingabe und Ausdauer zu dem gleichen Berufe
beseelt, dieselben äußeren Lebensschicksale, wie
schon oben erwähnt.

From 1816 onwards, the brothers experienced the same
external fate as mentioned above, inspired by the same
dedication and perseverance for the same profession.

Wilhelm G. starb am 16, Dezember 1859 in Berlin.   3.5

Wilhelm G. died in Berlin on December 16, 1859.

Während sein Bruder Jacob unvermählt geblieben   3.6
ist,

While his brother Jacob remained unmarried,

war Wilhelm G. verheiratet: 3.7

Wilhelm G. was married:

ein Sohn von ihm ist der noch lebende Berliner   3.8
Kunsthistoriker Hermann Grimm, der Verfasser
des Michelangelo, der Vorlesungen über Goethe und
zahlreicher Essays, deren stilistische Vornehmheit
auf das geistige Erbe des Vaters hindeutet.

one of his sons is the still living Berlin art historian
Hermann Grimm, the author of Michelangelo, the lectures
on Goethe and numerous essays, whose stylistic nobility
points to his father's intellectual heritage.

Von selbständig herausgegebenen Arbeiten W.   3.9
Grimms sind u. a. zu nennen:

Among W. Grimm's independently published works are:

»Altdänische Heldenlieder, Balladen und Märchen«   3.10
(1811);

"Altdänische Heldenlieder, Balladen und Märchen" (1811);

»Die deutsche Heldensage« (1829) und   3.11

"Die deutsche Heldensage" (1829) and

3.12 »Zur geschichte des reims« (1852).
"Zur geschichte des rims" (1852).

4.1 Von beiden Brüdern ist ohne Zweifel der ältere der bedeutendere.
Of the two brothers, the older is undoubtedly the more important.

4.2 Unterstützt von einem reichen Anschauungsvermögen, rasch und glücklich im Zusammenfassen von noch so weit auseinander liegenden Thatsachen und Gegenständen, kam er leicht zu den
Supported by a rich power of perception, quick and happy in summarizing facts and objects, no matter how far apart, he easily arrived at the

4.3 »bedeutungsvollsten Resultaten«, während die eigentliche Kritik, wie sie ein Lachmann und Haupt bewiesen, bei seiner poetischen Veranlagung weniger stark ausgeprägt war.
"most meaningful results", while the actual criticism, as demonstrated by Lachmann and Haupt, was less pronounced in his poetic disposition.

4.4 Die ungezwungene Lebendigkeit,
The unforced liveliness,

4.5 die volkstümliche Frische und Anschaulichkeit seiner Sprache verleiht ihm für immer einen Ehrenplatz unter den Meistern deutscher Prosa.
the popular freshness and vividness of his language will forever give him a place of honor among the masters of German prose.

Wilhelm G. war nicht von der gleichen tiefen
Ursprünglichkeit und Fruchtbarkeit;

4.6

Wilhelm G. was not of the same profound originality and
fertility;

aber seinem wahrhaft poetischen Empfinden und
seinem Verständnis für die Ausdrucksweise des
Volkes ist es zu verdanken,

4.7

but it is thanks to his truly poetic feeling and his
understanding of the people's way of expression that,

daß neben den »Deutschen Sagen«, besonders die

4.8

alongside the "German Legends", especially the

»Kinder - und Hausmärchen«, ein echtes Hausbuch
für die deutsche Kinderwelt geworden und geblieben
sind, die seit ihrem Erscheinen (1812) gleich den
Sternen noch nichts von ihrem ursprünglichen
Glanze verloren haben.

4.9

"Children's and Household Tales", have become and
remained a real house book for the German children's
world, which, like the stars, have lost nothing of their
original splendor since their publication (1812).

Hier ist der naive Ton des deutschen
Märchenerzählers in von anderen nie wieder
erreichter Weise getroffen.

4.10

Here the naive tone of the German storyteller has been
captured in a way never again achieved by others.

4.11 **Was die deutschen Romantiker, wie z. B. Tieck in seinen Phantasus-Geschichten, seiner Genoveva u. s. w. vergeblich erstrebten, die deutsch volkstümliche, schlichte Klarheit, unbewußte Gedankentiefe und wunderbare Plastik der Sprache, das finden wir in den Grimmschen**

What the German Romantics, such as Tieck in his Phantasus stories, his Genoveva, etc., strove for in vain, the German folkloric, simple clarity, unconscious depth of thought and wonderful sculpture of language, we find in the Grimm

4.12 **»Kinder - und Hausmärchen«.**

"Children's and Household Tales".

4.13 **Kein anderes Volk kann diesem Buche ein in seiner Gattung ähnliches an die Seite stellen.**

No other nation can match this book in its genre.

4.14 **Es ist auch klassisch,**

It is also classical,

4.15 **wenn klassisch nicht mehr bedeuten soll als vollendet in seiner Art.**

if classical does not mean more than perfect in its kind.

4.16 **Nicht mit Unrecht bemerkt ein neuerer Literarhistoriker, daß diese Märchen,**

It is not without reason that a recent literary historian remarks that these fairy tales

4.17 **»als Muster volksmäßiger Darstellung wohl für alle Zeiten unübertrefflich bleiben werden.«**

"will probably remain unsurpassable for all time as a model of popular representation."

Die späteren Ausgaben der »Kinder - und Hausmärchen«

5.1

The later editions of the "Children's and Household Tales"

sind von dem oben bereits genannten Hermann Grimm besorgt worden, der in pietätvollem Verständnis ihnen die Zueignung an Bettina von Arnim aus dem Jahre 1843 wieder vorangestellt hat.

5.2

were produced by the aforementioned Hermann Grimm, who, with reverent understanding, again prefixed them with the dedication to Bettina von Arnim from 1843.

Auch wir halten sie für unzertrennlich von dem wertvollen Buche und lassen sie hier folgen.

5.3

We, too, consider it inseparable from the valuable book and include it here.

Marienkind

Child of Mary

1.1 Vor einem großen Walde lebte ein Holzhacker mit seiner Frau, der hatte nur ein einziges Kind, das war ein Mädchen von drei Jahren.

Outside a large forest there lived a woodcutter with his wife, who had only one child, a girl of three.

1.2 Sie waren aber so arm, daß sie nicht mehr das tägliche Brot hatten und nicht wußten, was sie ihm sollten zu essen geben.

But they were so poor that they no longer had their daily bread, and did not know what to give him to eat.

1.3 Eines Morgens ging der Holzhacker voller Sorgen hinaus in den Wald an seine Arbeit, und wie er da Holz hackte, stand auf einmal eine schöne große Frau vor ihm, die hatte eine Krone von leuchtenden Sternen auf dem Haupt und sprach zu ihm:

One morning the wood-chopper went out into the forest to his work, full of cares, and as he was chopping wood, a beautiful tall woman suddenly stood before him, with a crown of shining stars on her head, and said to him:

1.4 »Ich bin die Jungfrau Maria,

"I am the Virgin Mary,

13

die Mutter des Christkindleins;   1.5
the mother of the infant Christ;

du bist arm und dürftig, bring mir dein Kind, ich   1.6
will es mit mir nehmen, seine Mutter sein und für es
sorgen.
you are poor and needy, bring me your child, and I will take
it with me, be its mother, and take care of it.

Der Holzhacker gehorchte, holte sein Kind und   1.7
übergab es der Jungfrau Maria, die nahm es mit
sich hinauf in den Himmel.
The woodcutter obeyed, took his child and gave it to the
Virgin Mary, who took it up with her to heaven.

Da ging es ihm wohl, es aß Zuckerbrot und trank   1.8
süße Mich, und seine Kleider waren von Gold, und
die Englein spielten mit ihm.
There he was well, he ate carrots and drank sweet milk, and
his clothes were of gold, and the angels played with him.

Als es nun vierzehn Jahre alt geworden war, rief es   1.9
einmal die Jungfrau Maria zu sich und sprach:
When she was fourteen years old, she once called the
Virgin Mary to her and said,

»Liebes Kind, ich habe eine große Reise vor, da   1.10
nimm die Schlüssel zu den dreizehn Thüren des
Himmelreichs in Verwahrung;
"Dear child, I have a great journey to make, so take the keys
of the thirteen doors of the kingdom of heaven into your
keeping;

1.11 zwölf davon darfst du aufschließen und die Herrlichkeiten darin betrachten, aber die dreizehnte, wozu dieser kleine Schlüssel gehört, die ist dir verboten:

twelve of them you may unlock and behold the glories therein, but the thirteenth, to which this little key belongs, is forbidden to you:

1.12 hüte dich, daß du sie nicht aufschließest, sonst wirst du unglücklich.«

beware that you do not unlock it, or you will be unhappy."

1.13 Das Mädchen versprach gehorsam zu sein, und als nun die Jungfrau Maria weg war, fing sie an und besah die Wohnungen des Himmelreichs; jeden Tag schloß es eine auf, bis die zwölfe herum waren.

The girl promised to be obedient, and when the Virgin Mary was gone, she began to visit the apartments of the kingdom of heaven, unlocking one every day until the twelve were completed.

1.14 In jeder aber saß ein Apostel, und war von großem Glanz umgeben, und es freute sich über all die Pracht und Herrlichkeit, und die Englein, die es immer begleiteten, freuten sich mit ihm.

But in each sat an apostle, and was surrounded by great splendor, and he rejoiced in all the splendor and glory, and the angels who always accompanied him rejoiced with him.

1.15 Nun war die verbotene Thür allein noch übrig, da empfand es eine große Lust zu wissen, was dahinter verborgen wäre, und sprach zu den Englein:

Now the forbidden door alone was left, and she felt a great desire to know what was hidden behind it, and said to the angels,

»Ganz aufmachen will ich sie nicht und will auch nicht hineingehen, aber ich will sie aufschließen, damit wir ein wenig durch den Ritz sehen.«   1.16

"I will not open it all the way, nor will I go in, but I will unlock it, that we may see a little through the crack."

»Ach nein.« sagten die Englein, »das wäre Sünde;   1.17

"Oh no." said the little angels, "that would be a sin;

die Jungfrau Maria hat's verboten,   1.18

the Virgin Mary has forbidden it,

und es könnte leicht dein Unglück werden.«   1.19

and it might easily be your misfortune."

Da schwieg es still, aber die Begierde in seinem Herzen schwieg nicht still, sondern nagte und pickte ordentlich daran und ließ ihm keine Ruhe.   1.20

Then he was silent, but the desire in his heart was not silent, but gnawed and pecked at it and left him no peace.

Und als die Englein einmal alle hinausgegangen waren, dachte es   1.21

And once the little angels had all gone out, she thought,

»Nun bin ich ganz allein und könnte hineingucken, es weiß es ja niemand, wenn ich's thue.«   1.22

"Now I am all alone and could look in, no one would know if I did."

Es suchte den Schlüssel heraus und als es ihn in der Hand hielt, steckte es ihn auch in das Schloß, und als es ihn hineingesteckt hatte, drehte es auch um.   1.23

She looked for the key, and when she had it in her hand, she put it into the lock, and when she had put it in, she turned it.

1.24 **Da sprang die Thür auf,**
Then the door burst open,

1.25 **und es sah da die Dreieinigkeit im Feuer und Glanz sitzen.**
and she saw the Trinity sitting there in fire and splendor.

1.26 **Es blieb ein Weilchen stehen und betrachtete alles mit Erstaunen, dann rührte es ein wenig mit dem Finger an den Glanz, da ward der Finger ganz golden.**
She stood still for a little while and looked at everything with astonishment, then she touched the glow a little with her finger, and her finger became quite golden.

1.27 **Alsbald empfand es eine gewaltige Angst,**
Immediately she felt a tremendous fear,

1.28 **schlug die Thür zu und lief fort.**
slammed the door and ran away.

1.29 **Die Angst wollte auch nicht wieder weichen, es mochte anfangen, was es wollte, und das Herz klopfte in einem fort und wollte nicht ruhig werden;**
The fear would not leave her again, she could do what she liked, and her heart beat all the time and would not calm down;

1.30 **auch das Gold blieb an dem Finger und ging nicht ab,**
the gold also remained on her finger and would not come off,

1.31 **es mochte waschen und reiben so viel es wollte.**
she could wash and rub it as much as she liked.

2.1 **Gar nicht lange,**
Not long after,

so kam die Jungfrau Maria von ihrer Reise zurück.   2.2
the Virgin Mary returned from her journey.

Sie rief das Mädchen zu sich und forderte ihm die   2.3
Himmelsschlüssel wieder ab.
She called the girl to her and asked her for the keys to
heaven.

Als es den Bund hinreichte, blickte ihm die Jungfrau   2.4
in die Augen, und sprach:
When she handed over the covenant, the Virgin looked her
in the eye and said:

»Hast du auch nicht die dreizehnte Thür geöffnet?«   2.5
"Have you not opened the thirteenth door?"

»Nein.« antwortete es.   2.6
"No." she answered.

Da legte sie ihre Hand auf sein Herz, fühlte wie es   2.7
klopfte und klopfte, und merkte wohl, daß es ihr
Gebot übertreten und die Thür aufgeschlossen hatte.
Then she laid her hand on his heart, felt it beating and
beating, and realized that he had transgressed her
commandment and had unlocked the door.

Da sprach sie noch einmal: »Hast du es gewiß nicht   2.8
gethan?«
Then she said again: "Did you not do it?"

»Nein.« sagte das Mädchen zum zweitenmal.   2.9
"No." said the girl a second time.

2.10 Da erblickte sie den Finger, der von der Berührung des himmlischen Feuers golden geworden, war, sah wohl, daß es gesündigt hatte und sprach zum drittenmal:

Then she caught sight of the finger, which had become golden from the touch of the heavenly fire, saw that she had sinned, and said for the third time:

2.11 »Hast du es nicht gethan?«

"Did you not do it?"

2.12 »Nein.« sagte das Mädchen, zum drittenmal.

"No." said the girl, for the third time.

2.13 Da sprach die Jungfrau Maria:

Then the Virgin Mary said,

2.14 »Du hast mir nicht gehorcht, und hast noch dazu gelogen, du bist nicht mehr würdig im Himmel zu sein.«

"You have disobeyed me, and you have also lied; you are no longer worthy to be in heaven."

3.1 Da versank das Mädchen in einen tiefen Schlaf, und als es erwachte, lag es unten auf der Erde, mitten in einer Wildnis.

Then the girl sank into a deep sleep and when she woke up, she was lying on the ground in the middle of a wilderness.

3.2 Es wollte rufen, aber es konnte keinen Laut hervorbringen.

She wanted to call out, but she could not make a sound.

Es sprang auf und wollte fortlaufen, aber wo es sich hinwendete, immer ward es von dichten Dornhecken zurückgehalten, die es nicht durchbrechen konnte.   3.3

She jumped up and wanted to run away, but wherever she turned, she was always held back by dense thorn hedges that she could not break through.

In der Einöde, in welche es eingeschlossen war, stand ein alter hoher Baum, das mußte seine Wohnung sein.   3.4

There was an old tall tree in the wasteland where it was trapped, which must have been its home.

Da kroch es hinein, wenn die Nacht kam, und schlief darin, und wenn es stürmte und regnete, fand es darin Schutz;   3.5

She crept into it when night came, and slept in it, and when it stormed and rained she found shelter in it;

aber es war ein jämmerliches Leben, und wenn es daran dachte, wie es im Himmel so schön gewesen war, und die Engel mit ihm gespielt hatten, so weinte es bitterlich.   3.6

but it was a miserable life, and when she thought of how beautiful it had been in heaven, and how the angels had played with her, she wept bitterly.

Wurzeln und Waldbeeren waren seine einzige Nahrung, die suchte es sich, soweit es kommen konnte.   3.7

Roots and wild berries were her only food, and she sought them as far as she could.

3.8 Im Herbst sammelte es die herabgefallenen Nüsse und Blätter und trug sie in die Höhle, die Nüsse waren im Winter seine Speise, und wenn Schnee und Eis kam, so kroch es wie ein armes Tierchen in die Blätter, daß es nicht fror.

In the fall she gathered the fallen nuts and leaves and carried them into the cave, the nuts were her food in winter, and when snow and ice came she crawled into the leaves like a poor little animal so that she would not freeze.

3.9 **Nicht lange,**

Before long,

3.10 so zerrissen seine Kleider und fiel ein Stück nach dem andern vom Leibe herab.

his clothes tore and fell off his body one piece at a time.

3.11 Sobald dann die Sonne wieder warm schien, ging es heraus und setzte sich vor den Baum, und seine langen Haare bedeckten es von allen Seiten wie ein Mantel.

As soon as the sun shone warmly again, he went out and sat down in front of the tree, and his long hair covered him on all sides like a cloak.

3.12 So saß es ein Jahr nach dem andern und fühlte den Jammer und das Elend der Welt.

She sat like this for year after year, feeling the misery and misery of the world.

Einmal, als die Bäume wieder in frischem Grün
standen, jagte der König des Landes in dem Walde
und verfolgte ein Reh, und weil es in das Gebüsch
geflohen war, das den Waldplatz einschloß, stieg er
vom Pferd, riß das Gestrüppe auseinander und hieb
sich mit seinem Schwert einen Weg.

4.1

Once, when the trees were green again, the king of the
country was hunting in the forest, pursuing a deer,
and because it had fled into the bushes that enclosed
the wooded area, he dismounted his horse, tore the
undergrowth apart and cut his way through with his
sword.

Als er endlich hindurchgedrungen war, sah er unter
dem Baum ein wunderschönes Mädchen sitzen, das
saß da und war von seinem goldenen Haar bis zu den
Fußzehen bedeckt.

4.2

When he had finally made his way through, he saw a
beautiful girl sitting under the tree with her golden hair
down to her toes.

Er stand still und betrachtete es voll Erstaunen, dann
redete er es an und sprach:

4.3

He stood still and looked at her in astonishment, then he
spoke to her and said,

»Wer bist du? warum sitzest du hier in der Einöde?«

4.4

"Who are you? why are you sitting here in the wasteland?"

Es gab aber keine Antwort,

4.5

But it gave no answer,

denn es konnte seinen Mund nicht aufthun.

4.6

for it could not open its mouth.

Der König sprach weiter,

4.7

The king continued,

4.8 »Willst du mit mir auf mein Schloß gehen?«
"Will you go with me to my castle?"

4.9 Da nickte es nur ein wenig mit dem Kopf.
He nodded his head a little.

4.10 Der König nahm es auf seinen Arm, trug es auf
sein Pferd und ritt mit ihm heim, und als er auf das
königliche Schloß kam, ließ er ihm schöne Kleider
anziehen und gab ihm alles im Überfluß.
The King took him in his arms, carried him on his horse,
and rode home with him, and when he came to the royal
palace, he had him dressed in beautiful clothes, and gave
him everything in abundance.

4.11 Und ob es gleich nicht sprechen konnte, so war es
doch schön und holdselig, daß er es von Herzen lieb
gewann, und es dauerte nicht lange, da vermählte er
sich mit ihm.
And though she could not speak, yet she was beautiful
and lovely, so that he loved her dearly, and it was not long
before he married her.

5.1 Als etwa ein Jahr verflossen war,
When about a year had passed,

5.2 brachte die Königin einen Sohn zur Welt.
the queen gave birth to a son.

5.3 Darauf in der Nacht, wo sie allein in ihrem Bette lag,
erschien ihr die Jungfrau Maria und sprach:
Then at night, as she lay alone in her bed, the Virgin Mary
appeared to her and said:

»Willst du die Wahrheit sagen und gestehen, daß 5.4
du die verbotene Thür aufgeschlossen hast, so
will ich deinen Mund öffnen und dir die Sprache
wiedergeben;

"If you will tell the truth and confess that you have opened
the forbidden door, I will open your mouth and restore
your speech;

verharrst du aber in der Sünde und leugnest 5.5
hartnäckig,

but if you persist in sin and stubbornly deny it,

so nehme ich dein neugebornes Kind mit mir.« 5.6

I will take your newborn child with me."

Da war der Königin verliehen zu antworten, sie blieb 5.7
aber verstockt und sprach,

Then the queen was lent to answer, but she remained
obstinate and said,

»Nein, ich habe die verbotene Thür nicht 5.8
aufgemacht.«

"No, I have not opened the forbidden door."

und die Jungfrau Maria nahm das neugeborene Kind 5.9
ihr aus den Armen und verschwand damit.

and the Virgin Mary took the newborn child from her arms
and disappeared with it.

Am anderen Morgen, als das Kind nicht zu finden 5.10
war, ging ein Gemurmel unter den Leuten, die
Königin wäre eine Menschenfresserin und hätte
ihr eigenes Kind umgebracht.

The next morning, when the child was nowhere to be
found, there was a murmur among the people that the
queen was a man-eater and had killed her own child.

5.11 **Sie hörte alles und konnte nichts dagegen sagen, der König aber wollte es nicht glauben, weil er sie so lieb hatte.**

She heard everything and could say nothing against it, but the king refused to believe it because he loved her so much.

6.1 **Nach einem Jahr gebar die Königin wieder einen Sohn.**

After a year the queen again gave birth to a son.

6.2 **In der Nacht trat auch wieder die Jungfrau Maria zu ihr herein und sprach:**

That night the Virgin Mary came to her again and said,

6.3 **»Willst du gestehen, daß du die verbotene Thür geöffnet hast, so will ich dir dein Kind wiedergeben und deine Zunge lösen;**

"If you will confess that you have opened the forbidden door, I will give you back your child and loose your tongue;

6.4 **verharrst du aber in der Sünde und leugnest,**

but if you persist in sin and deny it,

6.5 **so nehme ich auch dieses neugeborene mit mir.«**

I will also take this newborn child with me."

6.6 **Da sprach die Königin wiederum: »Nein,**

Then the queen said again, "No,

6.7 **ich habe die verbotene Thür nicht geöffnet.«**

I have not opened the forbidden door."

6.8 **und die Jungfrau nahm ihr das Kind aus den Armen weg und mit sich in den Himmel.**

and the maiden took the child from her arms and took him with her to heaven.

Am Morgen, als das Kind abermals verschwunden war, sagten die Leute ganz laut, die Königin hätte es verschlungen, und des Königs Räte verlangten, daß sie sollte gerichtet werden.

6.9

In the morning, when the child had again disappeared, the people said very loudly that the queen had devoured it, and the king's counselors demanded that she should be judged.

Der König aber hatte sie so lieb, daß er es nicht glauben wollte, und befahl den Räten, bei Leibes - und Lebensstrafe nichts mehr darüber zu sprechen.

6.10

But the king was so fond of her that he would not believe it, and ordered the councillors to say no more about it, under penalty of life and limb.

Im nächsten Jahre gebar die Königin ein schönes Töchterlein,

7.1

The next year the queen gave birth to a beautiful little daughter,

da erschien ihr zum drittenmal nachts die Jungfrau Maria und sprach:

7.2

when the Virgin Mary appeared to her for the third time at night and said:

»Folge mir.«

7.3

"Follow me."

Sie nahm sie bei der Hand und führte sie in den Himmel, und zeigte ihr da ihre beiden ältesten Kinder, die lachten sie an und spielten mit der Weltkugel.

7.4

She took her by the hand and led her to heaven, and there showed her her two eldest children, who laughed at her and played with the globe.

7.5 Als sich die Königin darüber freute, sprach die Jungfrau Maria,

When the Queen rejoiced at this, the Virgin Mary said,

7.6 »Ist dein Herz noch nicht erweicht?

"Is not thy heart yet softened?

7.7 wenn du eingestehst, daß du die verbotene Thür geöffnet hast, so will ich dir deine beiden Söhnlein zurückgeben.«

if thou wilt confess that thou hast opened the forbidden door, I will give thee back thy two little sons."

7.8 Aber die Königin antwortete zum drittenmal: »Nein,

But the queen answered for the third time, "No,

7.9 ich habe die verbotene Thür nicht geöffnet.«

I have not opened the forbidden door."

7.10 Da ließ sie die Jungfrau wieder zur Erde hinabsinken und nahm ihr auch das dritte Kind.

Then she let the maiden sink down to the ground again and took the third child from her.

8.1 Am anderen Morgen, als es ruchbar ward, riefen alle Leute laut,

The next morning, when it became known, all the people cried aloud,

8.2 »Die Königin ist eine Menschenfresserin,

"The queen is a man-eater,

8.3 sie muß verurteilt werden.«

she must be condemned."

und der König konnte seine Räte nicht mehr
zurückweisen.

8.4

and the king could no longer refuse his counsel.

Es ward ein Gericht über sie gehalten, und weil sie
nicht antworten und sich nicht verteidigen konnte,
ward sie verurteilt, auf dem Scheiterhaufen zu
sterben.

8.5

A judgment was held on her, and because she could not
answer or defend herself, she was condemned to die at the
stake.

Das Holz wurde zusammengetragen, und als sie
an einen Pfahl festgebunden war und das Feuer
ringsumher zu brennen anfing, da schmolz das harte
Eis des Stolzes und ihr Herz ward von Reue bewegt,
und sie dachte:

8.6

The wood was gathered together, and when she was tied to
a stake and the fire began to burn all around her, the hard
ice of pride melted and her heart was moved with remorse,
and she thought,

»Könnt ich nur noch vor meinem Tode gestehen, daß
ich die Thür geöffnet habe.«

8.7

"If only I could confess before I die that I opened the door."

da kam ihr die Stimme, daß sie laut ausrief:

8.8

Then the voice came to her that she exclaimed aloud:

»Ja, Maria, ich habe es gethan!«

8.9

"Yes, Mary, I have done it!"

8.10 **Und alsbald fing der Himmel an zu regnen und löschte die Feuerflammen, und über ihr brach ein Licht hervor, und die Jungfrau Maria kam herab und hatte die beiden Söhnlein zu ihren Seiten und das neugeborene Töchterlein auf dem Arm.**

And immediately the sky began to rain and extinguished the flames of fire, and a light burst forth above her, and the Virgin Mary came down with the two little sons at her sides and the new-born daughter in her arms.

8.11 **Sie sprach freundlich zu ihr:**

She spoke kindly to her:

8.12 **»Wer seine Sünde bereut und eingesteht, dem ist sie vergeben.«**

"Whoever repents and confesses his sin is forgiven."

8.13 **und reichte ihr die drei Kinder,**

and handed her the three children,

8.14 **löste ihr die Zunge und gab ihr Glück für das ganze Leben.**

untied her tongue and gave her happiness for life.

Märchen vom einem, der auszog das Fürchten zu lernen

Fairy Tale of one who set out to learn to fear

1.1 Ein Vater hatte zwei Söhne, davon war der älteste klug und gescheit, und wußte sich in alles wohl zu schicken, der jüngste aber war dumm, konnte nichts begreifen und lernen: und wenn ihn die Leute sahen, sprachen sie,

A father had two sons, of whom the eldest was clever and clever, and knew how to do everything well, but the youngest was stupid, could not understand or learn anything: and when people saw him, they said,

1.2 »Mit dem wird der Vater noch seine Last haben!«

"His father will have his work cut out for him!"

1.3 Wenn nun etwas zu thun war,

Now if there was something to be done,

1.4 so mußte es der älteste allezeit ausrichten;

the eldest had to do it all the time;

hieß ihn aber der Vater noch spät oder gar in der   1.5
Nacht etwas holen, und der Weg ging dabei über
den Kirchhof oder sonst einen schaurigen Ort, so
antwortete er wohl:
but if his father told him to fetch something late or even at
night, and the way went through the churchyard or some
other scary place, he would probably answer:

»Ach nein, Vater, ich gehe nicht dahin, es gruselt   1.6
mir!«
"Oh no, father, I'm not going there, it scares me!"

denn er fürchtete sich.   1.7
because he was afraid.

Oder, wenn abends beim Feuer Geschichten erzählt   1.8
wurden, wobei einem die Haut schaudert, so
sprachen die Zuhörer manchmal:
Or, when stories were told by the fire in the evening that
made your skin crawl, the listeners would sometimes say:

»Ach, es gruselt mir!«   1.9
"Oh, it's scary!"

Der jüngste saß in einer Ecke und hörte das mit an,   1.10
und konnte nicht begreifen was es heißen sollte.
The youngest sat in a corner and listened to this and
couldn't understand what it meant.

»Immer sagen sie es gruselt mir!   1.11
"They always say it gives me the creeps!

es gruselt mir! mir gruselt's nicht;   1.12
it gives me the creeps! it doesn't give me the creeps;

1.13 das wird wohl eine Kunst sein, von der ich auch nichts verstehe.«

that must be an art I don't understand either."

2.1 Nun geschah es, daß der Vater einmal zu ihm sprach:

Now it happened that his father once said to him:

2.2 »Hör du, in der Ecke dort, du wirst groß und stark, du mußt auch etwas lernen, womit du dein Brot verdienst.

"Listen, in that corner there, you are growing up and getting strong, you must learn something to earn your bread.

2.3 Siehst du, wie dein Bruder sich Mühe giebt, aber an dir ist Hopfen und Malz verloren.«

You see how hard your brother is trying, but you're a lost cause."

2.4 »Ei, Vater.« antwortete er,

"Oh, father." he answered,

2.5 »ich will gerne was lernen; ja, wenn's anginge, so möchte ich lernen, daß mir's gruselte: davon verstehe ich noch gar nichts.«

"I should like to learn something; yes, if I could, I should like to learn so much that it would frighten me; I don't know anything about it yet."

2.6 Der älteste lachte, als er das hörte, und dachte bei sich:

The eldest laughed when he heard this, and thought to himself,

»Du lieber Gott, was ist mein Bruder ein Dummbart, aus dem wird sein Lebtag nichts; 2.7

"Dear God, what a fool my brother is, he won't amount to anything for the rest of his life;

was ein Häkchen werden will, muß sich bei Zeiten krümmen.« 2.8

if he wants to be a little boy, he must bend in time."

Der Vater seufzte und antwortete ihm: 2.9

His father sighed and said to him,

»Das Gruseln, das sollst du schon lernen, aber dein Brot wirst du damit nicht verdienen.« 2.10

"You shall learn to be scary, but you won't earn your living with it."

Bald danach kam der Küster zum Besuch ins Haus, da klagte ihm der Vater seine Not und erzählte, wie sein jüngster Sohn in allen Dingen so schlecht beschlagen wäre, er wüßte nichts und lernte nichts. 3.1

Soon afterwards, the sexton came to the house for a visit, and the father complained to him about his misery and told him how his youngest son was so poorly versed in all things, that he knew nothing and learned nothing.

»Denkt Euch, als ich ihn fragte, womit er sein Brot verdienen wollte, hat er gar verlangt, das Gruseln zu lernen.« 3.2

"Think about it, when I asked him what he wanted to do for a living, he even asked to learn how to scare."

»Wenn's weiter nichts ist.« antwortete der Küster, 3.3

"If it's nothing else." replied the sexton,

»das kann er bei mir lernen; thut ihn nur zu mir, 3.4

"he can learn that from me; just bring him to me,

3.5 ich werde ihn schon abhobeln.« Der Vater war es zufrieden,

I'll pick him up." The father was pleased,

3.6 weil er dachte:

for he thought:

3.7 »der Junge wird doch ein wenig zugestutzt.«

"The boy will be a little cut up after all."

3.8 Der Küster nahm ihn also ins Haus,

So the sexton took him into the house,

3.9 und er mußte die Glocke läuten.

and he had to ring the bell.

3.10 Nach ein paar Tagen weckte er ihn um Mitternacht, hieß ihn aufstehen, in den Kirchturm steigen und läuten.

After a few days, he woke him up at midnight, told him to get up, climb into the church tower and ring the bell.

3.11 »Du sollst schon lernen, was Gruseln ist.«

"You should learn what it means to be creepy."

3.12 dachte er, ging heimlich voraus, und als der Junge oben war und sich umdrehte und das Glockenseil fassen wollte, so sah er auf der Treppe, dem Schallloch gegenüber, eine weiße Gestalt stehen.

he thought, and went ahead secretly, and when the boy was upstairs and turned around to grab the bell rope, he saw a white figure standing on the stairs opposite the sound hole.

3.13 »Wer da?«

"Who's there?"

rief er, aber die Gestalt gab keine Antwort, regte und bewegte sich nicht.

he called out, but the figure gave no answer, did not move or stir.

3.14

»Gieb Antwort.« rief der Junge,

"Answer me." shouted the boy,

3.15

»oder mache, daß du fort kommst, du hast hier in der Nacht nichts zu schaffen.«

"or get out of here, you have no business here at night."

3.16

Der Küster aber blieb unbeweglich stehen,

But the sexton remained motionless,

3.17

damit der Junge glauben sollte es wäre ein Gespenst.

so that the boy would think it was a ghost.

3.18

Der Junge rief zum zweitenmal: »Was willst du hier?

The boy called out for the second time, "What do you want here?

3.19

Sprich, wenn du ein ehrlicher Kerl bist oder ich werfe dich die Treppe hinab.«

Speak up if you're an honest fellow or I'll throw you down the stairs."

3.20

Der Küster dachte: »Das wird so schlimm nicht gemeint sein.«

The sexton thought, "That won't be so bad."

3.21

gab keinen Laut von sich und stand, als wenn er von Stein wäre.

He made no sound and stood as if he were made of stone.

3.22

3.23 Da rief ihn der Junge zum drittenmale an, und als das auch vergeblich war, nahm er einen Anlauf und stieß das Gespenst die Treppe hinab, daß es zehn Stufen hinabfiel und in einer Ecke liegen blieb.

Then the boy called to him for the third time, and when this was also in vain, he took a run and pushed the ghost down the stairs so that it fell down ten steps and remained lying in a corner.

3.24 Darauf läutete er die Glocke, ging heim, legte sich, ohne ein Wort zu sagen, ins Bett und schlief fort.

Then he rang the bell, went home, lay down in bed without saying a word, and slept away.

3.25 Die Küsterfrau wartete lange Zeit auf ihren Mann,

The sexton's wife waited a long time for her husband,

3.26 aber er wollte nicht wiederkommen.

but he would not come back.

3.27 Da ward ihr endlich angst, sie weckte den Jungen, und fragte,

Then she finally became afraid, woke the boy and asked,

3.28 »Weißt du nicht, wo mein Mann geblieben ist?

"Don't you know where my husband has gone?

3.29 Er ist vor dir auf den Turm gestiegen.«

He climbed the tower before you did."

3.30 »Nein.« antwortete der Junge,

"No." replied the boy,

»aber da hat einer dem Schallloch gegenüber auf der Treppe gestanden, und weil er keine Antwort geben und auch nicht weggehen wollte, so habe ich ihn für einen Spitzbuben gehalten und hinuntergestoßen.

3.31

"but there was someone standing on the stairs opposite the sound hole, and because he wouldn't answer and wouldn't go away, I took him for a rascal and pushed him down.

Geht nur hin, so werdet Ihr sehen, ob er's gewesen ist, es sollte mir leid thun.«

3.32

Go and see if it was him, I should be sorry."

Die Frau sprang fort und fand ihren Mann, der in einer Ecke lag und jammerte, und ein Bein gebrochen hatte.

3.33

The woman jumped away and found her husband lying in a corner, wailing, with a broken leg.

Sie trug ihn herab und eilte dann mit lautem Geschrei zu dem Vater des Jungen.

4.1

She carried him down and then rushed to the boy's father, shouting loudly.

»Euer Junge.« rief sie,

4.2

"Your boy." she cried,

»hat ein großes Unglück angerichtet, meinen Mann hat er die Treppe hinabgeworfen, daß er ein Bein gebrochen hat:

4.3

"he has done a great mischief, he has thrown my husband down the stairs and broken his leg:

schafft den Taugenichts aus unserem Hause.«

4.4

get that good-for-nothing out of our house."

Der Vater erschrak,

4.5

The father was startled,

38

4.6 kam herbeigelaufen und schalt den Jungen aus.
came running up and scolded the boy.

4.7 »Was sind das für gottlose Streiche,
"What ungodly pranks these are,

4.8 die muß dir der Böse eingegeben haben.«
the Evil One must have put them in your head."

4.9 »Vater.« antwortete er, »hört nur an,
"Father." he answered, "listen to me,

4.10 ich bin ganz unschuldig:
I am quite innocent:

4.11 er stand da in der Nacht, wie einer, der Böses im Sinne hat.
he stood there in the night like one who has evil in mind.

4.12 Ich wußte nicht wer's war,
I did not know who it was,

4.13 und habe ihn dreimal ermahnt zu reden oder wegzugehen.«
and I warned him three times to speak or go away."

4.14 »Ach.«
"Alas."

4.15 sprach der Vater, »mit dir erleb' ich nur Unglück, geh' mir aus den Augen, ich will dich nicht mehr ansehen.«
said the father, "I have only bad luck with you, get out of my sight, I don't want to look at you any more."

4.16 »Ja.
"Yes.

Vater, recht gerne, wartet nur bis es Tag ist, da will ich ausgehen und das Gruseln lernen, so versteh ich doch eine Kunst, die mich ernähren kann.«

Father, I'd love to, just wait until it's daylight, then I want to go out and learn how to scare, so I can understand an art that can feed me."

4.17

»Lerne was du willst.« sprach der Vater,

"Learn what you like." said his father,

4.18

»mir ist alles einerlei.

"it's all the same to me.

4.19

Da hast du fünfzig Thaler, damit geh' in die weite Welt und sage keinem Menschen, wo du her bist und wer dein Vater ist, denn ich muß mich deiner schämen.«

There you have fifty thalers, go into the wide world with them, and tell no one where you come from or who your father is, for I must be ashamed of you."

4.20

»Ja, Vater, wie Ihr's haben wollt, wenn Ihr nicht mehr verlangt, das kann ich leicht in acht behalten.«

"Yes, father, how you want it, if you don't ask for more, I can easily keep that in mind."

4.21

Als nun der Tag anbrach, steckte der Junge seine fünfzig Thaler in die Tasche, ging hinaus auf die große Landstraße und sprach immer vor sich hin:

When day broke, the boy put his fifty thalers in his pocket, and went out into the high road, saying to himself,

5.1

»Wenn mir's nur gruselte! wenn mir's nur gruselte!«

"If only I were frightened! if only I were frightened!"

5.2

5.3 Da kam ein Mann heran, der hörte das Gespräch, das der Junge mit sich selber führte, und als sie ein Stück weiter waren, daß man den Galgen sehen konnte, sagte der Mann zu ihm:

Then a man came along, who overheard the conversation the boy was having with himself, and when they were a little way off, so that they could see the gallows, the man said to him,

5.4 »Siehst du, dort ist der Baum, wo sieben mit des Seilers Tochter Hochzeit gehalten haben und jetzt das Fliegen lernen;

"See, there is the tree where seven of them married the roper's daughter, and are now learning to fly;

5.5 setz dich darunter und warte, bis die Nacht kommt, so wirst du schon das Gruseln lernen.«

sit down under it, and wait till night comes, and you will learn to be creepy."

5.6 »Wenn weiter nichts dazu gehört.« antwortete der Junge,

"If there is nothing more to it." answered the boy,

5.7 »das ist leicht gethan;

"that is easily done;

5.8 lerne ich aber so geschwind das Gruseln,

but if I learn to scare so quickly,

5.9 so sollst du meine fünfzig Thaler haben;

you shall have my fifty thalers;

5.10 komm nur morgen früh wieder zu mir.«

only come to me again in the morning."

Da ging der Junge zu dem Galgen, setzte sich
darunter und wartete, bis der Abend kam.   5.11
So the boy went to the gallows, sat down under it and
waited until evening came.

Und weil ihn fror, machte er sich ein Feuer an;   5.12
And because he was cold, he lit a fire;

aber um Mitternacht ging der Wind so kalt, daß er   5.13
trotz des Feuers nicht warm werden wollte.
but at midnight the wind was so cold that he would not get
warm in spite of the fire.

Und als der Wind die Gehenkten gegeneinander stieß,   5.14
daß sie sich hin und her bewegten, so dachte er,
And when the wind knocked the hanged men against each
other, so that they moved to and fro, he thought,

»du frierst unten bei dem Feuer,   5.15
"You are freezing down below by the fire,

was mögen die da oben erst frieren und zappeln.«   5.16
what might they be freezing and fidgeting up there."

Und weil er mitleidig war, legte er die Leiter an, stieg   5.17
hinauf, knüpfte einen nach dem anderen los, und
holte sie alle sieben herab.
And because he was compassionate, he put on the ladder,
climbed up, untied them one by one, and brought them all
seven down.

Darauf schürte er das Feuer, blies es an und setzte sie   5.18
ringsherum, daß sie sich wärmen sollten.
Then he stoked the fire, blew on it, and set them all around
to warm themselves.

Aber sie saßen da und regten sich nicht,   5.19
But they sat there and did not move,

5.20 **und das Feuer ergriff ihre Kleider.**
and the fire took hold of their clothes.

5.21 **Da sprach er: »Nehmt euch in acht, sonst häng' ich euch wieder hinauf.«**
Then he said, "Take care, or I will hang you up again."

5.22 **Die Toten aber hörten nicht,**
But the dead did not listen,

5.23 **schwiegen und ließen ihre Lumpen fortbrennen.**
remained silent and let their rags burn away.

5.24 **Da ward er bös und sprach:**
Then he became angry and said,

5.25 **»Wenn ihr nicht acht geben wollt, so kann ich euch nicht helfen, ich will nicht mit euch verbrennen.«**
"If you won't be careful, I can't help you, I won't burn with you."

5.26 **und hing sie nach der Reihe wieder hinauf.**
and hung them up again in turn.

5.27 **Nun setzte er sich zu seinem Feuer und schlief ein, und am anderen Morgen, da kam der Mann zu ihm, wollte die fünfzig Thaler haben und sprach,**
Then he sat down by his fire and fell asleep, and the next morning the man came to him, wanted the fifty thalers, and said,

5.28 **»Nun, weißt du was gruseln ist?«**
"Well, do you know what horror is?"

5.29 **»Nein.« antwortete er, »woher sollte ich's wissen?**
"No." he replied, "how should I know?

Die da droben haben das Maul nicht aufgethan und
waren so dumm, daß sie die paar alten Lappen, die sie
am Leibe haben, brennen ließen.«
They didn't open their mouths up there, and were so stupid
that they let the few old rags they had on their bodies
burn."

5.30

Da sah der Mann, daß er die fünfzig Thaler heute
nicht davontragen würde, ging fort und sprach,
Then the man saw that he would not get away with the fifty
thalers today, and went away, saying,

5.31

»So einer ist mir noch nicht vorgekommen.«
"I have never met such a fellow."

5.32

Der Junge ging auch seines Weges und fing wieder an
vor sich hin zu reden:
The boy also went on his way and began to talk to himself
again:

6.1

»Ach, wenn mir's nur gruselte; ach,
"Oh, if only I was frightened; oh,

6.2

wenn mir's nur gruselte!«
if only I was frightened!"

6.3

Das hörte ein Fuhrmann, der hinter ihm herschritt,
und fragte:
A carter who was walking behind him heard this and
asked:

6.4

»Wer bist du?«
"Who are you?"

6.5

»Ich weiß nicht.« antwortete der Junge.
"I don't know." replied the boy.

6.6

6.7 Der Fuhrmann fragte weiter: »Wo bist du her?«
The carter continued: "Where are you from?"

6.8 »Ich weiß nicht.«
"I don't know."

6.9 »Wer ist dein Vater?«
"Who is your father?"

6.10 »Das darf ich nicht sagen.«
"I'm not allowed to say."

6.11 »Was brummst du beständig in den Bart hinein?«
"What are you constantly muttering into your beard?"

6.12 »Ei.« antwortete der Junge,
"Egg." answered the boy,

6.13 »ich wollte, daß mir's gruselte, aber niemand kann mir's lehren.«
"I wanted to be frightened, but no one can teach me."

6.14 »Laß dein dummes Geschwätz.«
"Stop your foolish talk."

6.15 sprach der Fuhrmann, »komm, geh' mit mir, ich will sehen, daß ich dich unterbringe.«
said the carter, "come, go with me, I will see that I put you up."

6.16 Der Junge ging mit dem Fuhrmann, und abends gelangten sie zu einem Wirtshaus, wo sie übernachten wollten.
The boy went with the carter, and in the evening they came to an inn where they intended to spend the night.

Da sprach er beim Eintritt in die Stube wieder ganz laut: 6.17
As they entered the parlor, he said again very loudly,

»Wenn mir's nur gruselte: wenn mir's nur gruselte!« 6.18
"If only I were frightened, if only I were frightened!"

Der Wirt, der das hörte, lachte und sprach: 6.19
The innkeeper, who heard this, laughed and said:

»Wenn dich danach lüstet, 6.20
"If that's what you want,

dazu sollte hier wohl Gelegenheit sein.« 6.21
there should be an opportunity here."

»Ach schweig stille.« sprach die Wirtsfrau, 6.22
"Oh, keep quiet." said the innkeeper's wife,

»so mancher Vorwitzige hat schon sein Leben eingebüßt, es wäre Jammer und Schade um die schönen Augen, wenn die das Tageslicht nicht wieder sehen sollten.« 6.23
"many a cheeky one has already lost his life, it would be a pity and a shame for the beautiful eyes if they should not see the light of day again."

Der Junge aber sagte: 6.24
But the boy said,

»Wenn's noch so schwer wäre, ich will's einmal lernen, deshalb bin ich ja ausgezogen.« 6.25
"No matter how hard it is, I want to learn, that's why I went out."

6.26 Er ließ dem Wirt auch keine Ruhe, bis dieser erzählte, nicht weit davon stände ein verwünschtes Schloß, wo einer wohl lernen könnte was gruseln wäre, wenn er nur drei Nächte darin wachen wollte.

He gave the innkeeper no peace until he told him that there was a haunted castle not far away, where someone could learn what it meant to be creepy if he only wanted to stay there for three nights.

6.27 Der König hätte dem, der's wagen wollte, seine Tochter zur Frau versprochen, und die wäre die schönste Jungfrau, welche die Sonne beschien;

The king had promised his daughter as a wife to anyone who dared, and she would be the most beautiful maiden the sun could shine on;

6.28 in dem Schlosse steckten auch große Schätze, von bösen Geistern bewacht, die würden dann frei und könnten einen Armen reich genug machen.

the castle also contained great treasures, guarded by evil spirits, which would then be set free and could make a poor man rich enough.

6.29 Schon viele wären wohl hinein,

Many had already gone in,

6.30 aber noch keiner wieder herausgekommen.

but none had yet come out.

6.31 Da ging der Junge am anderen Morgen vor den König und sprach,

So the boy went before the king the next morning and said,

6.32 »Wenn's erlaubt wäre,

"If it were permitted,

so wollte ich wohl drei Nächte in dem verwünschten Schlosse wachen.«

6.33

I would watch over the cursed castle for three nights."

Der König sah ihn an, und weil er ihm gefiel, sprach er:

6.34

The king looked at him, and because he liked him, he said,

»Du darfst dir noch dreierlei ausbitten, aber es müssen leblose Dinge sein, und das darfst du mit ins Schloß nehmen.«

6.35

"You may ask for three more things, but they must be inanimate objects, and you may take them into the castle with you."

Da antwortete er: »So bitt' ich um ein Feuer, eine Drehbank und eine Schnitzbank mit dem Messer.«

6.36

He replied, "I will ask for a fire, a lathe and a carving bench with a knife."

Der König ließ ihm das alles bei Tage in das Schloß tragen.

7.1

The king had all this carried into the castle by day.

Als es Nacht werden wollte, ging der Junge hinauf, machte sich in einer Kammer ein Helles Feuer an, stellte die Schnitzbank mit dem Messer daneben und setzte sich auf die Drehbank.

7.2

When night fell, the boy went up, lit a bright fire in a chamber, put the carving bench with the knife next to it and sat down on the lathe.

»Ach, wenn mir's nur gruselte!« sprach er,

7.3

"Oh, if only I was scared!" he said,

»aber hier werde ich's auch nicht lernen.«

7.4

"but I won't learn it here either."

48

7.5 Gegen Mitternacht wollte er sich sein Feuer einmal aufschüren:

Towards midnight, he wanted to stoke up his fire:

7.6 wie er so hineinblies,

as he was blowing into it,

7.7 da schrie's plötzlich aus einer Ecke: »Au, miau!

there was a sudden cry from a corner: "Ow, meow!

7.8 was uns friert!«

What's freezing!"

7.9 »Ihr Narren.« rief er, »was schreit ihr?

"You fools." he shouted, "what are you shouting about?

7.10 Wenn euch friert, kommt, setzt euch ans Feuer und wärmt euch.«

If you're cold, come and sit by the fire and warm yourselves."

7.11 Und wie er das gesagt hatte, kamen zwei große schwarze Katzen in einem gewaltigen Sprunge herbei, letzten sich ihm zu beiden Seiten, und sahen ihn mit ihren feurigen Augen ganz wild an.

And as soon as he had said this, two great black cats came running up in a mighty leap, came to either side of him, and looked at him wildly with their fiery eyes.

7.12 Über ein Weilchen, als sie sich gewärmt hatten, sprachen sie,

After a while, when they had warmed themselves, they said,

7.13 »Kamerad, wollen wir eins in der Karte spielen?«

"Comrade, shall we play one in the card?"

»Warum nicht?« antwortete er,   7.14
"Why not?" he replied,

»aber zeigt einmal eure Pfoten her.«   7.15
"but let's see your paws."

Da streckten sie die Krallen aus. »Ei.« sagte er, 7.16
Then they stretched out their claws. "Egg." he said,

»was habt ihr lange Nägel: wartet,   7.17
"what long nails you have: wait,

die muß ich euch erst abschneiden!«   7.18
I'll have to cut them off first!"

Damit packte er sie beim Kragen,   7.19
With that he grabbed them by the collar,

hob sie auf die Schnitzbank und schraubte ihnen die   7.20
Pfoten fest.
lifted them onto the carving bench and screwed their paws
tight.

»Euch habe ich auf die Finger, gesehen.« sprach er, 7.21
"I've seen you on your fingers." he said,

»da vergeht mir die Lust zum Kartenspiel.«   7.22
"and I've lost my appetite for playing cards."

schlug sie tot und warf sie hinaus ins Wasser.   7.23
He beat them to death and threw them out into the water.

7.24 Als er aber die zwei zur Ruhe gebracht hatte und sich wieder zu seinem Feuer setzen wollte, da kamen aus allen Ecken und Enden, schwarze Katzen und schwarze Hunde an glühenden Ketten, immer mehr und mehr, daß er sich nicht mehr bergen konnte;

But when he had put the two to rest, and was about to sit down by his fire again, black cats and black dogs on glowing chains came from all quarters, more and more, so that he could no longer hide himself;

7.25 die schrien greulich, traten ihm auf sein Feuer, zerrten es auseinander und wollten es ausmachen.

they screamed horribly, trod on his fire, tore it apart, and wanted to put it out.

7.26 Das sah er ein Weilchen ruhig mit an, als es ihm aber zu arg ward, faßte er sein Schnitzmesser und rief:

He watched this calmly for a while, but when it got too bad for him, he grabbed his carving knife and shouted:

7.27 »Fort mit dir, du Gesindel.« und haute auf sie los.

"Away with you, you riff-raff." and he cut at them.

7.28 Ein Teil sprang weg,

Some of them jumped away,

7.29 die anderen schlug er tot und warf sie hinaus in den Teich.

the others he beat to death and threw them out into the pond.

7.30 Als er wieder, gekommen war, blies er aus den Funken sein Feuer frisch an und wärmte sich.

When he came back, he blew a fresh fire from the sparks and warmed himself.

7.31 Und als er so saß,

And as he sat there,

wollten ihm die Augen nicht länger offen bleiben und er bekam Lust zu schlafen.

7.32

his eyes no longer wanted to stay open and he felt like sleeping.

Da blickte er um sich und sah in der Ecke ein großes Bett:

7.33

Then he looked around and saw a large bed in the corner:

»Das ist mir eben recht.« sprach er und legte sich hinein.

7.34

"That's just fine with me." he said and lay down in it.

Als er aber die Augen zuthun wollte,

7.35

But as he was about to close his eyes,

so fing das Bett von selbst an zu fahren und fuhr im ganzen Schloß herum.

7.36

the bed began to move of its own accord and moved all around the castle.

»Recht so.« sprach er, »nur besser zu.«

7.37

"That's right." he said, "only better close it."

Da rollte das Bett fort, als wären sechs Pferde vorgespannt, über Schwellen und Treppen auf und ab;

7.38

Then the bed rolled away as if it were harnessed to six horses, up and down over thresholds and stairs;

auf einmal hopp hopp! warf es um, das unterste zu oberst, daß es wie ein Berg auf ihm lag.

7.39

all at once, chop-chop, it toppled over, the bottom one to the top, so that it lay on it like a mountain.

7.40 Aber er schleuderte Decken und Kissen in die Höhe, stieg heraus und sagte,
But he flung blankets and pillows up into the air, got out, and said,

7.41 »Nun mag fahren wer Lust hat.«
"Now, whoever wants to ride may do so."

7.42 legte sich an sein Feuer und schlief, bis es Tag war.
He lay down by his fire and slept till daylight.

7.43 Am Morgen kam der König, und als er ihn da auf der Erde liegen sah, meinte er, die Gespenster hätten ihn umgebracht, und er wäre tot.
In the morning the king came, and when he saw him lying there on the ground, he thought the ghosts had killed him and he was dead.

7.44 Da sprach er: »Es ist doch schade um den schönen Menschen.«
Then he said, "It is a pity about the beautiful man."

7.45 Das hörte der Junge, richtete sich auf und sprach:
The boy heard this, straightened up and said:

7.46 »So weit ist's noch nicht!«
"It's not that far yet!"

7.47 Da verwunderte sich der König, freute sich aber, und fragte wie es ihm gegangen wäre.
The king was astonished, but rejoiced and asked how he had fared.

7.48 »Recht gut.« antwortete er, »eine Nacht wäre herum,
"Quite well." he replied, "one night will be over,

7.49 die zwei anderen werden auch herumgehen.«
and the other two will also be over."

Als er zum Wirt kam, da machte der große Augen.   7.50
When he came to the innkeeper, his eyes widened.

»Ich dachte nicht.« sprach er,   7.51
"I did not think." said he,

»daß ich dich wieder lebendig sehen würde;   7.52
"that I should see you alive again;

hast du nun gelernt, was Gruseln ist?«   7.53
have you now learned what horror is?"

»Nein.« sagte er, »es ist alles vergeblich;   7.54
"No." he said, "it is all in vain;

wenn mir's nur einer sagen könnte!«   7.55
if only someone could tell me!"

Die zweite Nacht ging er abermals hinaus ins alte   8.1
Schloß,
The second night he went out again to the old castle,

setzte sich zum Feuer und fing sein altes Lied   8.2
wieder an:
sat down by the fire and began his old song again:

»Wenn mir's nur gruselte!«   8.3
"If only I was creeped out!"

8.4 Wie Mitternacht herankam, ließ sich ein Lärm und Gepolter hören, erst sachte, dann immer stärker, dann war's ein bißchen still, endlich kam mit lautem Geschrei ein halber Mensch den Schornstein herab und fiel vor ihm hin.

As midnight approached, there was a noise and a rumbling, at first gentle, then stronger and stronger, then it was a little quiet, and at last half a man came down the chimney with a loud cry and fell before him.

8.5 »Heda!« rief er, »noch ein halber gehört dazu,

"Heda!" he shouted, "another half belongs to it,

8.6 das ist zu wenig.«

that's not enough."

8.7 Da ging der Lärm von frischem an, es tobte und heulte, und fiel die ändere Hälfte auch herab.

Then the noise of a fresh one began, it raged and howled, and the other half also fell down.

8.8 »Wart'.« sprach er,

"Wait." said he,

8.9 »ich will dir erst das Feuer ein wenig anblasen.«

"I will first blow the fire a little for you."

8.10 Wie er das gethan hatte und sich wieder umsah, da waren die beiden Stücke zusammengefahren und saß da ein greulicher Mann auf seinem Platz.

When he had done so, and looked round again, the two pieces had fallen together, and there sat a hideous man in his place.

8.11 »So haben wir nicht gewettet.« sprach der Junge,

"We didn't bet like that." said the boy,

»die Bank ist mein.« 8.12
"the bench is mine."

Der Mann wollte ihn wegdrängen, aber der Junge 8.13
ließ sich's nicht gefallen, schob ihn mit Gewalt weg
und setzte sich wieder auf seinen Platz.
The man tried to push him away, but the boy would not
stand for it, pushed him away by force and sat down in his
place again.

Da fielen noch mehr Männer herab, einer nach 8.14
dem andern, die holten neun Totenbeine und zwei
Totenköpfe, setzten auf und spielten Kegel.
Then more men fell down, one after the other, picked up
nine skulls and two skulls' heads, sat down and played
skittles.

Der Junge bekam auch Lust und fragte: »Hört ihr, 8.15
The boy also took a fancy to it and asked: "Listen,

kann ich mit sein?« 8.16
can I join you?"

»Ja, wenn du Geld hast.« 8.17
"Yes, if you have money."

»Geld genug.« antwortete er, 8.18
"Money enough." he replied,

»aber eure Kugeln sind nicht recht rund.« 8.19
"but your balls aren't quite round."

Da nahm er die Totenköpfe, 8.20
So he took the skulls,

setzte sie in die Drehbank und drehte sie rund. »So, 8.21
put them in the lathe and turned them round. "There,

8.22 jetzt werden sie besser schüppeln.« sprach er, »heida!
now they'll be better." he said, "heida!

8.23 nun geht's lustig!«
now it's fun!"

8.24 Er spielte mit und verlor etwas von seinem Geld, als es aber zwölf schlug, war alles vor seinen Augen verschwunden.
He played along and lost some of his money, but when the clock struck twelve, it had all disappeared before his eyes.

8.25 Er legte sich nieder und schlief ruhig ein.
He lay down and fell asleep peacefully.

8.26 Am anderen Morgen kam der König und wollte sich erkundigen.
The next morning, the king came to inquire.

8.27 »Wie ist dir's diesmal gegangen?« fragte er.
"How did you do this time?" he asked.

8.28 »Ich habe gekegelt.« antwortete er,
"I bowled." he replied,

8.29 »und ein paar Heller verloren.«
"and lost a few pennies."

8.30 »Hat dir denn nicht gegruselt?«
"Didn't you get the creeps?"

8.31 »Ei was.« sprach er, »lustig hab ich mich gemacht.
"Well." he said, "I had fun.

8.32 Wenn ich nur wüßte was Gruseln wäre?«
If only I knew what scary was?"

In der dritten Nacht setzte er sich wieder auf seine Bank und sprach ganz verdrießlich: 9.1
On the third night, he sat down on his bench again and said quite morosely:

»Wenn es mir nur gruselte!« Als es spät ward, 9.2
"If only it gave me the creeps!" When it grew late,

kamen sechs große Männer und brachten eine Totenlade hereingetragen. 9.3
six tall men came and brought in a shroud.

Da sprach er: 9.4
Then he said,

»Ha ha, das ist gewiß mein Vetterchen, das erst vor ein paar Tagen gestorben ist.« 9.5
"Ha ha, that must be my cousin, who died only a few days ago."

winkte mit dem Finger und rief: »Komm, Vetterchen, komm!« 9.6
He waved his finger and called out, "Come, cousin, come!"

Sie stellten den Sarg auf die Erde, 9.7
They put the coffin on the ground,

er aber ging hinzu und nahm den Deckel ab: 9.8
but he went and took off the lid:

da lag ein toter Mann darin. Er fühlte ihm an's Gesicht, 9.9
there lay a dead man in it. He felt his face,

aber es war kalt wie Eis. »Wart'.« sprach er, 9.10
but it was as cold as ice. "Wait." he said,

9.11 »ich will dich ein bißchen wärmen.«

"I will warm you a little."

9.12 **ging ans Feuer, wärmte seine Hand und legte sie ihm auf's Gesicht, aber der Tote blieb kalt.**

He went to the fire, warmed his hand and put it on his face, but the dead man remained cold.

9.13 **Nun nahm er ihn heraus, setzte sich ans Feuer und legte ihn auf seinen Schoß, und rieb ihm die Arme, damit das Blut wieder in Bewegung kommen sollte.**

Now he took him out, sat down by the fire and laid him on his lap, and rubbed his arms to get the blood moving again.

9.14 **Als auch das nichts helfen wollte, fiel ihm ein,**

When that didn't help either, he remembered that

9.15 **»wenn zwei zusammen im Bett liegen, so wärmen sie sich.«**

"when two people lie in bed together, they warm each other."

9.16 **brachte ihn ins Bett, deckte ihn zu und legte sich neben ihn.**

He took him to bed, covered him up and lay down next to him.

9.17 **Über ein Weilchen ward auch der Tote warm und fing an sich zu regen.**

After a while, the dead man warmed up and began to stir.

9.18 **Da sprach der Junge: »Siehst du, Vetterchen, hätt' ich dich nicht gewärmt!«**

Then the boy said, "You see, cousin, if I hadn't warmed you!"

9.19 **Der Tote aber hob an und rief,**

But the dead man raised his head and cried,

»Jetzt will ich dich erwürgen.« 9.20
"Now I want to strangle you."

»Was.« sagte er, »ist das mein Dank? 9.21
"What." he said, "is that my thanks?

Gleich sollst du wieder in deinen Sarg.« hub ihn auf, 9.22
You shall be back in your coffin in a moment." He
lifted it up,

warf ihn hinein und machte den Deckel zu; 9.23
threw it in and closed the lid;

da kamen die sechs Männer und trugen ihn wieder 9.24
fort.
then the six men came and carried it away again.

»Es will mir nicht gruseln.« sagte er, 9.25
"I don't want to be frightened." said he,

»hier lerne ich's mein Lebtag nicht.« 9.26
"I shall never learn it here for the rest of my life."

Da trat ein Mann herein, der war größer als alle 10.1
andere und sah fürchterlich aus;
Then a man came in who was taller than all the others and
looked terrible;

er war aber alt und hatte einen langen weißen Bart. 10.2
but he was old and had a long white beard.

»O du Wicht.« rief er. 10.3
"Oh, you wretch." he cried.

»nun sollst du bald lernen was Gruseln ist, 10.4
"Now you shall soon learn what horror is,

10.5 denn du sollst sterben.«

for you shall die."

10.6 »Nicht so schnell.« antwortete der Junge,

"Not so fast." answered the boy,

10.7 »soll ich sterben, so muß ich auch dabei sein.«

"if I am to die, I must be there too."

10.8 »Dich will ich schon packen.« sprach der Unhold.

"I want to grab you." said the ogre.

10.9 »Sachte, sachte, mach' dich nicht so breit;

"Easy, easy, don't spread yourself so wide;

10.10 so stark wie du bin ich auch, und wohl noch stärker.«

I'm as strong as you, and probably stronger."

10.11 »Das wollen wir sehen.« sprach der Alte,

"Let's see." said the old man,

10.12 »bist du stärker als ich, so will ich dich gehen lassen; komm,

"if you're stronger than me, I'll let you go; come on,

10.13 wir wollen's versuchen.«

let's give it a try."

10.14 Da führte er ihn durch dunkle Gänge zu einem Schmiedefeuer,

So he led him through dark corridors to a forge,

10.15 nahm eine Axt und schlug den einen Amboß mit einem Schlag in die Erde.

took an axe and smashed one of the anvils into the ground with one blow.

»Das kann ich noch besser.« sprach der Junge, 10.16
"I can do that even better." said the boy,

und ging zu dem anderen Amboß; 10.17
and went to the other anvil;

der Alte stellte sich neben hin und wollte zusehen, 10.18
the old man stood beside it and wanted to watch,

und sein weißer Bart hing herab. Da faßte der Junge 10.19
die Axt,
and his white beard drooped. Then the boy took the axe,

spaltete den Amboß auf einen Hieb und klemmte den 10.20
Bart den Alten mit hinein.
split the anvil in one stroke and jammed the old man's
beard into it.

»Nun hab' ich dich.« sprach der Junge, 10.21
"Now I've got you." said the boy,

»jetzt ist das Sterben an dir.« 10.22
"now it's your turn to die."

Dann faßte er eine Eisenstange und schlug auf 10.23
den Alten los, bis er wimmerte und bat, er möchte
aufhören, er wollte ihm große Reichtümer geben.
Then he seized an iron bar and struck the old man until he
whimpered and begged him to stop, he wanted to give him
great riches.

Der Junge zog die Axt raus und ließ ihn los. 10.24
The boy pulled out the axe and let him go.

10.25 Der Alte führte ihn wieder ins Schloß zurück und zeigte ihm in einem Keller drei Kasten voll Gold.
The old man led him back into the castle and showed him three chests full of gold in a cellar.

10.26 »Davon.« sprach er,
"Some of this." he said,

10.27 »ist ein Teil den Armen, der andere dem König, der dritte dein.«
"is for the poor, some for the king and some for you."

10.28 Indem schlug es zwölf und der Geist verschwand, also daß der Junge im Finstern stand.
Then twelve o'clock struck, and the ghost disappeared, so that the boy stood in darkness.

10.29 »Ich werde mir doch heraushelfen können.«
"I shall be able to help myself out."

10.30 sprach er, tappte herum, fand den Weg in die Kammer und schlief dort bei seinem Feuer ein.
said he, groped about, found his way into the chamber, and fell asleep there by his fire.

10.31 Am anderen Morgen kam der König und sagte:
The next morning, the king came and said:

10.32 »Nun wirst du gelernt haben was Gruseln ist?«
"Now you will have learned what scary is?"

10.33 »Nein.« antwortete er, »was ist's nur?
"No." he replied, "what is it?

Mein toter Vetter war da, und ein bärtiger Mann ist gekommen, der hat mir da unten viel Geld gezeigt, aber was Gruseln ist, hat mir keiner gesagt.«   10.34
My dead cousin was there, and a bearded man came and showed me a lot of money down there, but nobody told me what creepy is."

Da sprach der König: 10.35
Then the king said,

»Du hast das Schloß erlöst und sollst meine Tochter heiraten.«   10.36
"You have redeemed the castle and shall marry my daughter."

»Das ist alles recht gut.« antwortete er,   10.37
"That's all very well." he replied,

»aber ich weiß noch immer nicht was Gruseln ist.«   10.38
"but I still don't know what creepy is."

Da ward das Gold herausgebracht und die Hochzeit gefeiert, aber der junge König, so lieb er seine Gemahlin hatte und so vergnügt er war, sagte doch immer,   11.1
Then the gold was brought out and the wedding celebrated, but the young king, as fond as he was of his wife and as happy as he was, kept saying,

»Wenn mir nur gruselte; wenn mir nur gruselte.«   11.2
"If only I were frightened; if only I were frightened."

Das verdroß sie endlich. Ihr Kammermädchen sprach,   11.3
At last this annoyed her. Her chambermaid said,

11.4 »Ich will Hilfe schaffen, das Gruseln soll er schon lernen.«

"I will help him, he shall learn to be creepy."

11.5 Sie ging hinaus zum Bach, der durch den Garten floß und ließ sich einen ganzen Eimer voll Gründlinge holen.

She went out to the stream that flowed through the garden and fetched a whole bucketful of gudgeons.

11.6 Nachts, als der junge König schlief, mußte seine Gemahlin ihm die Decke wegziehen und den Eimer voll kaltes Wasser mit den Gründlingen über ihn herschütten, daß die kleinen Fische um ihn herumzappelten.

At night, when the young king was asleep, his wife had to pull the blanket off him and pour the bucket full of cold water with the gudgeons over him so that the little fish wriggled around him.

11.7 Da wachte er auf und rief,

Then he woke up and cried,

11.8 »Ach, was gruselt mir, was gruselt mir, liebe Frau! Ja,

"Oh, what a fright, what a fright, dear wife! Yes,

11.9 nun weiß ich was Gruseln ist.«

now I know what scary is."

Die Nixe im Teiche

The Mermaid in the Pond

1.1 **Es war einmal ein Müller, der führte mit seiner Frau ein vergnügtes Leben.**
Once upon a time there was a miller who led a happy life with his wife.

1.2 **Sie hatten Geld und Gut und ihr Wohlstand nahm von Jahr zu Jahr noch zu.**
They had money and goods and their prosperity increased from year to year.

1.3 **Aber Unglück kommt über Nacht;**
But misfortune comes overnight;

1.4 **wie ihr Reichtum gewachsen war, so schwand er von Jahr zu Jahr wieder hin, und zuletzt konnte der Müller kaum noch die Mühle, in der er saß, sein Eigentum nennen.**
just as their wealth had grown, so it dwindled from year to year, and in the end the miller could hardly call the mill in which he sat his own.

Er war voll Kummer, und wenn er sich nach der
Arbeit des Tages niederlegte, so fand er keine Ruhe,
sondern wälzte sich voll Sorgen in seinem Bett.

1.5

He was full of sorrow, and when he lay down after the day's
work, he found no rest, but tossed and turned in his bed full
of worry.

Eines Morgens stand er schon vor Tagesanbruch
auf, ging hinaus ins Freie und dachte, es sollte ihm
leichter ums Herz werden.

1.6

One morning he got up before dawn, went out into the open
air and thought his heart would be lighter.

Als er über den Mühldamm dahin schritt, brach eben
der erste Sonnenstrahl hervor, und er hörte in dem
Weiher etwas rauschen.

1.7

As he walked along the mill dam, the first ray of sunlight
broke through and he heard something rustling in the
pond.

Er wendete sich um und erblickte ein schönes Weib,
das sich langsam aus dem Wasser erhob.

1.8

He turned around and saw a beautiful woman slowly rising
from the water.

Ihre langen Haare, die sie über den Schultern mit
ihren zarten Händen gefaßt hatte, flossen an beiden
Seiten herab und bedeckten ihren weißen Leib.

1.9

Her long hair, which she had clasped over her shoulders
with her delicate hands, flowed down on either side and
covered her white body.

Er sah wohl, daß es die Nixe des Teiches war und
wußte vor Furcht nicht, ob er davongehen oder
stehen bleiben sollte.

1.10

He could see that it was the mermaid of the pond and was
afraid and did not know whether he should go away or
stand still.

1.11 Aber die Nixe ließ ihre sanfte Stimme hören, nannte ihn beim Namen und fragte, warum er so traurig wäre.

But the mermaid let her gentle voice be heard, called him by name and asked why he was so sad.

1.12 Der Müller war anfangs verstummt; als er sie aber so freundlich sprechen hörte, faßte er sich ein Herz und erzählte ihr, daß er sonst in Glück und Reichtum gelebt hätte, aber jetzt so arm wäre, daß er sich nicht zu raten wüßte.

The miller was silent at first, but when he heard her speak so kindly, he took heart and told her that he had otherwise lived in happiness and wealth, but was now so poor that he did not know what to do.

1.13 »Sei ruhig.« antwortete die Nixe,

"Be calm." replied the mermaid,

1.14 »ich will dich reicher und glücklicher machen als du je gewesen bist, nur mußt du mir versprechen, daß du mir geben willst, was eben in deinem Hause jung geworden ist.«

"I will make you richer and happier than you have ever been, only you must promise me that you will give me what has just become young in your house."

1.15 »Was kann das anders sein.« dachte der Müller,

"What else can that be." thought the miller,

1.16 »als ein junger Hund oder ein junges Kätzchen?«

"but a young dog or a young kitten?"

1.17 und sagte ihr zu, was sie verlangte.

and agreed to what she asked.

Die Nixe stieg wieder in das Wasser hinab und er eilte getröstet und gutes Mutes nach seiner Mühle.   1.18

The mermaid descended into the water again and he hurried back to his mill, comforted and in good spirits.

Noch hatte er sie nicht erreicht, da trat die Magd aus der Hausthür und rief ihm zu, er sollte sich freuen, seine Frau hätte ihm einen kleinen Knaben geboren.   1.19

He had not yet reached it when the maid stepped out of the house door and called out to him that he should be happy because his wife had given birth to a little boy.

Der Müller stand wie vom Blitz gerührt, er sah wohl, daß die tückische Nixe das gewußt und ihn betrogen hatte.   1.20

The miller stood as if moved by lightning; he could see that the treacherous mermaid had known this and had deceived him.

Mit gesenktem, Haupt trat er zu dem Bett seiner Frau, und als sie ihn fragte,   1.21

With bowed head he went to his wife's bedside, and when she asked him,

»Warum freust du dich nicht über den schönen Knaben?«,   1.22

"Why are you not happy about the beautiful boy?",

so erzählte er ihr, was ihm begegnet war und was für ein Versprechen er der Nixe gegeben hatte.   1.23

he told her what had happened to him and what promise he had made to the mermaid.

»Was hilft mir Glück und Reichtum.« fügte er hinzu,   1.24

"What good is happiness and wealth to me." he added,

1.25 »wenn ich mein Kind verlieren soll? Aber was kann ich thun?«
"if I am to lose my child? But what can I do?"

1.26 Auch, die Verwandten, die herbeigekommen waren, Glück zu wünschen, wußten keinen Rat.
Nor did the relatives who had come to wish him luck know what to do.

2.1 Indessen kehrte das Glück in das Haus des Müllers wieder ein.
Meanwhile, luck returned to the miller's house.

2.2 Was er unternahm, gelang, es war als ob Kisten und Kasten von selbst sich füllten und das Geld im Schrank über Nacht sich mehrte.
Everything he did succeeded, it was as if boxes and crates filled themselves and the money in the cupboard increased overnight.

2.3 Es dauerte nicht lange, so war sein Reichtum größer als je zuvor.
It wasn't long before his wealth was greater than ever before.

2.4 Aber er konnte sich nicht ungestört darüber freuen:
But he could not rejoice undisturbed:

2.5 die Zusage, die er der Nixe gethan hatte, quälte sein Herz.
the promise he had made to the mermaid tormented his heart.

2.6 So oft er an dem Teiche vorbei kam, fürchtete er, sie möchte auftauchen und ihn an seine Schuld mahnen.
As often as he passed the pond, he feared that she would appear and remind him of his guilt.

Den Knaben selbst ließ' er nicht in die Nähe des
Wassers: 2.7
He would not let the boy himself near the water:

»Hüte dich.« sagte er zu ihm,   2.8
"Beware." he said to him,

»wenn du das Wasser berührst, so kommt eine Hand   2.9
heraus, hascht dich und zieht dich hinab.«
"if you touch the water, a hand will come out, grab you and
pull you down."

Doch als Jahr auf Jahr verging, und die Nixe sich   2.10
nicht Wieder zeigte, so fing der Müller an sich zu
beruhigen.
But as year after year passed and the mermaid did not show
herself again, the miller began to calm down.

Der Knabe wuchs zum Jüngling heran und kam bei   3.1
einem Jäger in die Lehre.
The boy grew up to be a youth and was apprenticed to a
hunter.

Als er ausgelernt hatte und ein tüchtiger Jäger   3.2
geworden war,
When he had finished his apprenticeship and had become a
skilled hunter,

nahm ihn der Herr des Dorfes in seine Dienste.   3.3
the lord of the village took him into his service.

In dem Dorfe war ein schönes und treues Mädchen,   3.4
das gefiel dem Jäger, und als sein Herr das bemerkte,
schenkte er ihm ein kleines Haus;
There was a beautiful and faithful girl in the village who
pleased the hunter, and when his master noticed this, he
gave him a small house;

3.5 **die beiden hielten Hochzeit,**
the two of them got married,

3.6 **lebten ruhig und glücklich und liebten sich von Herzen.**
lived quietly and happily and loved each other dearly.

4.1 **Einstmals verfolgte der Jäger ein Reh.**
Once a hunter was chasing a deer.

4.2 **Als das Tier aus dem Walde in das freie Feld ausbog,**
When the animal turned out of the forest into the open field,

4.3 **setzte er ihm nach und streckte es endlich mit einem Schuß nieder.**
he pursued it and finally shot it down.

4.4 **Er bemerkte nicht, daß er sich in der Nähe des gefährlichen Weihers befand, und ging, nachdem er das Tier ausgeweidet hatte, zu dem Wasser, um seine mit Blut befleckten Hände zu waschen.**
He did not realize that he was near the dangerous pond and, after gutting the animal, went to the water to wash his blood-stained hands.

4.5 **Kaum aber hatte er sie hineingetaucht, als die Nixe emporstieg, lachend mit ihren nassen Armen ihn umschlang und so schnell hinabzog, daß die Wellen über ihm zusammenschlugen.**
But he had scarcely dipped them in when the mermaid rose up and, laughing, wrapped her wet arms around him and pulled him down so quickly that the waves crashed over him.

Als es Abend war und der Jäger nicht nach Hause kam,   5.1

When it was evening and the hunter did not come home,

so geriet seine Frau in Angst.   5.2

his wife became frightened.

Sie ging aus ihn zu suchen, und da er ihr oft erzählt hatte, daß er sich vor den Nachstellungen der Nixe in acht nehmen müßte und nicht in die Nähe des Weihers sich wagen dürfte, so ahnte sie schon, was geschehen war.   5.3

She went out to look for him, and as he had often told her that he must beware of the mermaid's pursuits, and must not venture near the pond, she already suspected what had happened.

Sie eilte zu dem Wasser, und als sie am Ufer seine Jägertasche fand, da konnte sie nicht länger an dem Unglück zweifeln.   5.4

She hurried to the water, and when she found his hunter's bag on the bank, she could no longer doubt his misfortune.

Wehklagend und händeringend rief sie ihren Liebsten mit Namen, aber vergeblich, sie eilte hinüber auf die andere Seite des Weihers, und rief ihn aufs neue, sie schalt die Nixe mit harten Worten, aber keine Antwort erfolgte.   5.5

Lamenting and wringing her hands, she called her beloved by name, but in vain, she hurried over to the other side of the pond and called him again, she scolded the mermaid with harsh words, but there was no answer.

5.6 **Der Spiegel des Wassers blieb ruhig, nur das halbe Gesicht des Mondes blickte unbeweglich zu ihr herauf.**

The mirror of the water remained still, only half the moon's face gazed up at her, unmoving.

6.1 **Die arme Frau verließ den Teich nicht.**

The poor woman did not leave the pond.

6.2 **Mit schnellen Schritten, ohne Rast und Ruhe, umkreiste sie ihn immer von neuem, manchmal still, manchmal einen heftigen Schrei ausstoßend, manchmal in leisem Wimmern.**

With quick steps, without rest or quiet, she circled it again and again, sometimes silently, sometimes uttering a fierce cry, sometimes whimpering softly.

6.3 **Endlich waren ihre Kräfte zu Ende:**

At last her strength ran out:

6.4 **sie sank zur Erde nieder und verfiel in einen tiefen Schlaf.**

she sank to the ground and fell into a deep sleep.

6.5 **Bald überkam sie ein Traum.**

Soon she was overcome by a dream.

7.1 **Sie stieg zwischen großen Felsblöcken angstvoll aufwärts:**

She climbed fearfully upwards between large boulders:

7.2 **Dornen und Ranken hakten sich an ihre Füße,**

thorns and vines clung to her feet,

der Regen schlug ihr ins Gesicht und der Wind zauste
ihr langes Haar.   7.3

the rain hit her in the face and the wind tousled her long
hair.

Als sie die Anhöhe erreicht hatte,   7.4

When she reached the top of the hill,

bot sich ein ganz anderer Anblick dar.   7.5

the view was completely different.

Der Himmel war blau, die Luft mild, der Boden   7.6
senkte sich sanft hinab und auf einer grünen, bunt
beblümten Wiese stand eine reinliche Hütte.

The sky was blue, the air was mild, the ground sloped
gently downwards and a clean hut stood on a green,
colorful flowered meadow.

Sie ging darauf zu und öffnete die Thür, da saß eine   7.7
Alte mit weißen Haaren, die ihr freundlich winkte.

She went up to it and opened the door, where an old
woman with white hair was sitting, beckoning to her in
a friendly manner.

In dem Augenblick erwachte die arme Frau.   7.8

At that moment the poor woman awoke.

Der Tag war schon angebrochen,   7.9

The day had already dawned,

und sie entschloß sich gleich dem Traume Folge zu   7.10
leisten.

and she decided to follow her dream.

Sie stieg mühsam den Berg hinauf, und es war alles   7.11
so, wie sie es in der Nacht, gesehen hatte.

She laboriously climbed the mountain, and everything was
just as she had seen it in the night.

7.12 **Die Alte empfing sie freundlich und zeigte ihr einen Stuhl, auf den sie sich setzen sollte.**
The old woman received her kindly and showed her a chair to sit on.

7.13 **»Du mußt ein Unglück erlebt haben.« sagte sie,**
"You must have had some misfortune." she said,

7.14 **»weil du meine einsame Hütte aufsuchst.«**
"because you have come to my lonely hut."

7.15 **Die Frau erzählte ihr unter Thränen, was ihr begegnet war.**
The woman tearfully told her what had happened to her.

7.16 **»Tröste dich.« sagte die Alte, »ich will dir helfen:**
"Take comfort." said the old woman, "I will help you:

7.17 **da hast du einen goldenen Kamm.**
there is a golden comb for you.

7.18 **Harre, bis der Vollmond aufgestiegen ist, dann geh' zu dem Weiher, setze dich am Rande nieder und strähle dein langes schwarzes Haar mit diesem Kamm.**
Wait until the full moon has risen, then go to the pond, sit down at the edge and comb your long black hair with this comb.

7.19 **Wenn du aber fertig bist, so lege ihn am Ufer nieder, und du wirst sehen was geschieht.«**
But when you have finished, lay it down on the bank and you will see what happens."

8.1 **Die Frau kehrte zurück,**
The woman returned,

aber die Zeit bis zum Vollmond verstrich ihr langsam.   8.2

but the time until the full moon passed slowly.

Endlich erschien die leuchtende Scheibe am Himmel;   8.3

At last the luminous disk appeared in the sky;

da ging sie hinaus an den Weiher, setzte sich nieder   8.4
und kämmte ihre langen schwarzen Haare mit dem
goldenen Kamm, und als sie fertig war, legte sie ihn
an den Rand des Wassers nieder.

then she went out to the pond, sat down and combed her
long black hair with the golden comb, and when she had
finished, she laid it down on the edge of the water.

Nicht lange, so brauste es aus der Tiefe, eine Welle   8.5
erhob sich, rollte an das Ufer und führte den Kamm
mit sich fort.

It was not long before a roar came from the depths, a wave
rose up, rolled onto the shore and carried the comb away
with it.

Es dauerte nicht länger, als der Kamm nötig   8.6
hatte, auf den Grund zu sinken, so teilte sich der
Wasserspiegel und der Kopf des Jägers stieg in die
Höhe.

It took no longer for the comb to sink to the bottom than
it took for the water level to part and the hunter's head to
rise.

Er sprach nicht,   8.7

He did not speak,

schaute aber seine Frau mit traurigen Blicken an.   8.8

but looked at his wife with a sad expression.

8.9 In demselben Augenblick kam eine zweite Welle
herangerauscht und bedeckte das Haupt des Mannes.
At the same moment, a second wave came rushing up and
covered the man's head.

8.10 Alles war verschwunden,
Everything had disappeared,

8.11 der Weiher lag so ruhig wie zuvor und nur das
Gesicht des Vollmondes glänzte darauf.
the pond lay as still as before and only the face of the full
moon shone on it.

9.1 Trostlos kehrte die Frau zurück,
The woman returned desolate,

9.2 doch der Traum zeigte ihr die Hütte der Alten.
but the dream showed her the old woman's hut.

9.3 Abermals machte sie sich am nächsten Morgen auf
den Weg und klagte der weisen Frau ihr Leid.
She set off again the next morning and complained to the
wise woman.

9.4 Die Alte gab ihr eine goldene Flöte und sprach:
The old woman gave her a golden flute and said:

9.5 »Harre, bis der Vollmond wieder kommt, dann nimm
diese Flöte, setze dich an das Ufer, blas ein schönes
Lied darauf, und wenn du damit fertig bist, so lege sie
auf den Sand;
"Wait until the full moon comes again, then take this flute,
sit down on the shore, blow a beautiful song on it, and
when you have finished, lay it on the sand;

9.6 du wirst sehen was geschieht.«
you will see what happens."

Die Frau that wie die Alte gesagt hatte.   9.7

The woman did as the old woman had said.

Kaum lag die Flöte auf dem Sand, so brauste es aus   9.8
der Tiefe:

No sooner had the flute been laid on the sand than there
was a roar from the depths:

eine Welle erhob sich,   9.9

a wave rose up,

zog heran und führte die Flöte mit sich fort.   9.10

drew near and carried the flute away with it.

Bald darauf teilte sich das Wasser und nicht bloß der   9.11
Kopf, auch der Mann bis zur Hälfte des Leibes stieg
hervor.

Soon after, the water parted and not only the head, but also
half of the man's body emerged.

Er breitete voll Verlangen seine Arme nach ihr aus,   9.12
aber eine zweite Welle rauschte heran, bedeckte ihn
und zog ihn wieder hinab.

Full of desire, he spread his arms out towards her, but a
second wave rushed in, covered him and pulled him down
again.

»Ach, was hilft es mir.« sagte die Unglückliche,   10.1

"Oh, what good will it do me." said the unhappy woman,

»daß ich, meinen Liebsten nur erblicke, um ihn   10.2
wieder zu verlieren.«

"that I should only see my beloved to lose him again."

Der Gram erfüllte aufs neue ihr Herz,   10.3

Grief filled her heart anew,

10.4 aber der Traum führte sie zum drittenmal in das Haus der Alten.

but the dream led her for the third time to the old woman's house.

10.5 Sie machte sich, auf den Weg und die weise Frau gab ihr ein goldenes Spinnrad, tröstete sie und sprach:

She set out, and the wise woman gave her a golden spinning-wheel, comforted her, and said,

10.6 »Es ist noch nicht alles vollbracht, harre, bis der Vollmond kommt, dann nimm das Spinnrad, setze dich an das Ufer und spinne die Spule voll, und wenn du fertig bist, so stelle das Spinnrad nahe an das Wasser und du wirst sehen was geschieht.«

"It is not all done yet, wait till the full moon comes, then take the spinning-wheel, sit down on the bank and spin the bobbin full, and when you have finished, place the spinning-wheel near the water, and you will see what happens."

11.1 Die Frau befolgte alles genau.

The woman followed everything exactly.

11.2 Sobald der Vollmond sich zeigte, trug sie das goldene Spinnrad an das Ufer und spann emsig, bis der Flachs zu Ende und die Spule mit dem Faden ganz angefüllt war.

As soon as the full moon appeared, she carried the golden spinning wheel to the shore and spun diligently until the flax was finished and the bobbin was completely filled with thread.

11.3 Kaum aber stand das Rad am Ufer,

But as soon as the wheel was on the shore,

so brauste es noch heftiger als sonst in der Tiefe des Wassers;   11.4
it roared even more violently than usual in the depths of the water;

eine mächtige Welle eilte herbei und trug das Rad mit sich fort.   11.5
a mighty wave rushed up and carried the wheel away with it.

Alsbald stieg mit einem Wasserstrahl der Kopf und der ganze Leib des Mannes in die Höhe.   11.6
Immediately the man's head and whole body rose up with a jet of water.

Schnell sprang er ans Ufer,   11.7
He quickly jumped to the shore,

faßte seine Frau an der Hand und entfloh.   11.8
grabbed his wife by the hand and fled.

Aber kaum hatten sie sich eine kleine Strecke entfernt, so erhob sich mit entsetzlichem Brausen der ganze Weiher und strömte mit reißender Gewalt in das weite Feld hinein.   11.9
But no sooner had they gone a short distance than the whole pond rose up with a terrible roar and flowed with tearing force into the wide field.

Schon sahen die Fliehenden ihren Tod vor Augen, da rief die Frau in ihrer Angst die Hilfe der Alten an, und in dem Augenblick waren sie verwandelt, sie in eine Kröte, er in einen Frosch.   11.10
The fleeing men already saw their death before their eyes, when the woman in her fear called for help from the old woman, and in an instant they were transformed, she into a toad, he into a frog.

11.11 **Die Flut, die sie erreicht hatte, konnte sie nicht töten, aber sie riß sie beide voneinander und führte sie weit weg.**

The flood that had reached them could not kill them, but it tore them both apart and led them far away.

12.1 **Als das Wasser sich verlaufen hatte und beide wieder den trockenen Boden berührten,**

When the water had gone and they both touched dry ground again,

12.2 **so kam ihre menschliche Gestalt zurück.**

their human form returned.

12.3 **Aber keiner wußte wo das andere geblieben war;**

But neither knew where the other had gone;

12.4 **sie befanden sich unter fremden Menschen, die ihre Heimat nicht kannten.**

they were among strangers who did not know their homeland.

12.5 **Hohe Berge und tiefe Thäler lagen zwischen ihnen.**

High mountains and deep valleys lay between them.

12.6 **Um sich das Leben zu erhalten, mußten beide die Schafe hüten.**

To keep themselves alive, they both had to herd sheep.

12.7 **Sie trieben lange Jahre ihre Herden durch Feld und Wald und waren voll Trauer und Sehnsucht.**

They drove their flocks through field and forest for many years and were full of grief and longing.

Als wieder einmal der Frühling aus der Erde
hervorgebrochen war, zogen beide an einem Tage
mit ihren Herden aus und der Zufall wollte, daß sie
einander entgegenzogen.

13.1

When spring had once more burst forth from the earth,
they both set out with their flocks one day, and chance
would have it that they went out to meet each other.

Er erblickte an einem fernen Bergesabhange eine
Herde und trieb seine Schafe nach der Gegend hin.

13.2

He caught sight of a flock on a distant mountain slope and
drove his sheep towards the area.

Sie kamen in einem Thal zusammen, aber sie
erkannten sich nicht, doch freuten sie sich, daß
sie nicht mehr so einsam waren.

13.3

They came together in a valley, but they did not recognize
each other, but they were glad that they were no longer so
lonely.

Von nun an trieben sie jeden Tag ihre Herde
nebeneinander;

13.4

From then on they drove their flocks side by side every day;

sie sprachen nicht viel, aber sie fühlten sich getröstet.

13.5

they did not talk much, but they felt comforted.

Eines Abends, als der Vollmond am Himmel schien
und die Schafe schon ruhten, holte der Schäfer die
Flöte aus seiner Tasche und blies ein schönes, aber
trauriges Lied.

13.6

One evening, when the full moon was shining in the sky
and the sheep were already resting, the shepherd took the
flute out of his pocket and played a beautiful but sad song.

13.7 **Als er fertig war, bemerkte er, daß die Schäferin bitterlich weinte.**

When he had finished, he noticed that the shepherdess was crying bitterly.

13.8 **»Warum weinst du?« fragte er. »Ach.« antwortete sie,**

"Why are you crying?" he asked. "Oh." she replied,

13.9 **»so schien auch der Vollmond, als ich zum letztenmal dieses Lied aus der Flöte blies und das Haupt meines Liebsten aus dem Wasser hervorkam.«**

"the full moon was shining when I blew that song from the flute for the last time and my beloved's head came out of the water."

13.10 **Er sah sie an und es war ihm, als fiele eine Decke von den Augen, er erkannte seine liebste Frau, und als sie ihn anschaute und der Mond aus sein Gesicht schien, erkannte sie ihn auch.**

He looked at her and it was as if a blanket fell from his eyes, he recognized his dearest wife, and when she looked at him and the moon shone from his face, she recognized him too.

13.11 **Sie umarmten und küßten sich, und ob sie glückselig waren, braucht keiner zu fragen.**

They embraced and kissed, and no one need ask if they were happy.

Die Geschenke des kleinen Volkes

The Gifts of the Little People

1.1 Ein Schneider und ein Goldschmied wanderten zusammen und vernahmen eines Abends, als die Sonne hinter die Berge gesunken war, den Klang einer fernen Musik, die immer deutlicher ward;

A tailor and a goldsmith were walking together, and one evening, when the sun had sunk behind the mountains, they heard the sound of a distant music, which became more and more distinct;

1.2 sie tönte ungewöhnlich, aber so anmutig, daß sie aller Müdigkeit vergaßen und rasch weiter schritten.

it sounded unusual, but so graceful that they forgot all weariness and walked on quickly.

Der Mond war schon aufgestiegen, als sie zu einem Hügel gelangten, auf dem sie eine Menge kleiner Männer und Frauen erblickten, die sich bei den Händen gefaßt hatten und mit größter Lust und Freudigkeit im Tänze herumwirbelten, sie sangen dazu auf das lieblichste; 1.3

The moon had already risen when they came to a hill, on which they saw a crowd of little men and women, who had joined hands and were whirling about in a dance with the greatest pleasure and joy, singing most sweetly;

und das war die Musik, die die Wanderer gehört hatten. 1.4

and this was the music the wanderers had heard.

In der Mitte saß ein Alter, der etwas größer war als die übrigen, der einen buntfarbigen Rock trug, und dem ein eisgrauer Bart über die Brust herabhing. 1.5

In the middle sat an old man, somewhat taller than the others, who wore a brightly colored skirt and had an ice-gray beard hanging down over his chest.

Die beiden blieben voll Verwunderung stehen und sahen dem Tanze zu. 1.6

The two stopped in amazement and watched the dance.

Der Alte winkte, sie sollten eintreten, und das kleine Volk öffnete bereitwillig seinen Kreis. 1.7

The old man beckoned them to enter, and the little people willingly opened their circle.

1.8 Der Goldschmied, der einen Höcker hatte und wie alle Buckligen keck genug war, trat herzu, der Schneider empfand zuerst einige Scheu und hielt sich zurück, doch als er sah, wie es so lustig herging, faßte er sich ein Herz und kam nach.

The goldsmith, who had a hump and was bold enough like all hunchbacks, came forward, the tailor felt a little shy at first and held back, but when he saw how much fun was being had, he took heart and joined in.

1.9 Alsbald, schloß sich der Kreis wieder und die Kleinen sangen und tanzten in den wildesten Sprüngen weiter.

The circle soon closed again and the little ones continued to sing and dance in the wildest leaps.

1.10 Der Alte aber nahm ein breites Messer, das an seinem Gürtel hing, wetzte es und als es hinlänglich geschärft war, blickte er sich nach den Fremdlingen um.

The old man, however, took a broad knife hanging from his belt, sharpened it and when it was sufficiently sharpened, he looked around at the strangers.

1.11 Es ward ihnen angst, aber sie hatten nicht lange Zeit sich zu besinnen, der Alte packte den Goldschmied und schor in der größten Geschwindigkeit ihm Haupthaar und Bart glatt hinweg;

They were frightened, but they did not have long to think things over;

1.12 ein gleiches geschah hierauf dem Schneider.

the old man seized the goldsmith and with the greatest speed shaved off his hair and beard, and did the same to the tailor.

Doch ihre Angst verschwand, als der Alte nach vollbrachter Arbeit beiden freundlich auf die Schulter klopfte, als wollte er sagen, sie hätten es gut gemacht, daß sie ohne Sträuben alles willig hätten geschehen lassen.

1.13

But their fear vanished when the old man patted them both kindly on the shoulder after the work was done, as if to say that they had done well, that they had willingly allowed everything to happen without resisting.

Er zeigte mit dem Finger auf einen Haufen Kohlen, der zur Seite lag, und deutete ihnen durch Gebärden an, daß sie ihre Taschen damit füllen sollten.

1.14

He pointed with his finger to a heap of coals lying to one side and gestured for them to fill their pockets with it.

Beide gehorchten, obgleich sie nicht wußten, wozu ihnen die Kohlen dienen sollten, und gingen dann weiter, um ein Nachtlager zu suchen.

1.15

Both obeyed, although they did not know what the coals were to be used for, and then went on to look for a place to camp for the night.

Als sie ins Thal gekommen waren,

1.16

When they had reached the valley,

schlug die Glocke des benachbarten Klosters zwölf Uhr:

1.17

the bell of the neighboring monastery struck twelve o'clock:

augenblicklich verstummte der Gesang,

1.18

immediately the singing stopped,

1.19 alles war verschwunden und der Hügel lag in einsamem Mondschein.

everything had disappeared and the hill lay in lonely moonlight.

2.1 Die beiden Wanderer fanden eine Herberge und deckten sich auf dem Strohlager mit ihren Röcken zu,

The two hikers found an inn and covered themselves with their skirts on the straw bed,

2.2 vergaßen aber wegen ihrer Müdigkeit die Kohlen zuvor herauszunehmen.

but forgot to take out the coals beforehand due to their tiredness.

2.3 Ein schwerer Druck auf ihren Gliedern weckte sie früher als gewöhnlich.

A heavy pressure on their limbs woke them up earlier than usual.

2.4 Sie griffen in die Taschen und wollten ihren Augen nicht trauen, als sie sahen, daß sie nicht mit Kohlen, sondern mit reinem Golde angefüllt waren;

They reached into their pockets and could not believe their eyes when they saw that they were not filled with coals, but with pure gold;

2.5 auch Haupthaar und Bart war glücklich wieder in aller Fülle vorhanden.

their hair and beards were also happily back in abundance.

Sie waren nun reiche Leute geworden, doch besaß   2.6
der Goldschmied, der seiner habgierigen Natur
gemäß die Taschen besser gefüllt hatte, noch einmal
so viel als der Schneider.

They had now become rich people, but the goldsmith, who,
in accordance with his greedy nature, had filled his pockets
better than the tailor.

Ein Habgieriger, wenn er viel hat, verlangt noch   2.7
mehr, der Goldschmied machte dem Schneider den
Vorschlag, noch einen Tag zu verweilen, am Abend
wieder hinauszugehen, um sich, bei dem Alten auf
dem Berge noch größere Schätze zu holen.

A greedy man, when he has a lot, wants even more; the
goldsmith suggested to the tailor that he should stay
another day and go out again in the evening to fetch even
greater treasures from the old man on the mountain.

Der Schneider wollte nicht und sagte: 2.8

The tailor refused and said:

»Ich habe genug und bin zufrieden, jetzt werde ich   2.9
Meister, heirate meinen angenehmen Gegenstand
(wie er seine Liebste nannte) und bin ein glücklicher
Mann.«

"I have had enough and am satisfied, now I will become
a master, marry my pleasant object (as he called his
sweetheart) and be a happy man."

Doch wollte er ihm zu Gefallen den Tag noch bleiben.   2.10

But he wanted to stay the day to please him.

Abends hing der Goldschmied noch ein paar Taschen   2.11
über die Schulter, um recht einsacken zu können,
und machte sich auf den Weg zu dem Hügel.

In the evening, the goldsmith hung a few bags over his
shoulder so that he could bag up properly and set off for the
hill.

2.12 Er fand, wie in der vorigen Nacht, das kleine Volk bei Gesang und Tanz, der Alte schor ihn abermals glatt und deutete ihm an, Kohlen mitzunehmen.

As on the previous night, he found the little people singing and dancing, and the old man again shushed him and told him to take some coal with him.

2.13 Er zögerte nicht, einzustecken was nur in seine Taschen gehen wollte, kehrte ganz glückselig heim und deckte sich mit dem Rock zu.

He did not hesitate to pocket what he wanted, returned home quite happy and covered himself with his skirt.

2.14 »Wenn das Gold auch drückt.« sprach er,

"Even if the gold is a burden." he said,

2.15 »ich will das schon ertragen.«

"I will bear it."

2.16 und schlief endlich mit dem süßen Vorgefühl ein, morgen als steinreicher Mann zu erwachen.

and finally fell asleep with the sweet anticipation of waking up tomorrow as a stone-rich man.

2.17 Als er die Augen öffnete, erhob er sich schnell, um die Taschen zu untersuchen;

When he opened his eyes, he rose quickly to examine his pockets;

2.18 aber wie erstaunte er, als er nichts herauszog als schwarze Kohlen, er mochte so oft hineingreifen als er wollte.

but how astonished he was when he pulled out nothing but black coals, which he could reach into as often as he liked.

2.19 »Noch bleibt mir das Gold, das ich die Nacht vorher gewonnen habe.«

"I still have the gold I won the night before."

dachte er und holte es herbei, aber wie erschrak er, als er sah, daß es ebenfalls wieder zu Kohle geworden war. 2.20

he thought, and fetched it, but how startled he was when he saw that it had also turned back into coal.

Er schlug sich mit der schwarzbestäubten Hand an die Stirn; da fühlte er, 2.21

He struck his forehead with his black-dusted hand,

daß der ganze Kopf kahl und glatt war wie das Gesicht. 2.22

and felt that his whole head was as bald and smooth as his face.

Aber sein Mißgeschick war noch nicht zu Ende, er merkte erst jetzt, daß ihm zu dem Höcker auf dem Rücken noch ein zweiter ebenso großer vorn auf der Brust gewachsen war. 2.23

But his misfortune was not yet at an end; he only now realized that in addition to the bump on his back, a second equally large one had grown on the front of his chest.

Da erkannte er die Strafe seiner Habgier und begann laut zu weinen. 2.24

Then he realized the punishment of his greed and began to weep aloud.

Der gute Schneider, der davon aufgeweckt ward, tröstete den Unglücklichen so gut es gehen wollte und sprach, 2.25

The good tailor, who was awakened by this, comforted the unfortunate man as best he could and said,

»Du bist mein Geselle auf der Wanderschaft gewesen, 2.26

"You have been my journeyman on his travels,

2.27 du sollst bei mir bleiben und mit von meinem Schatz zehren.«

you shall stay with me and feed on my treasure. "

2.28 Er hielt Wort,

He kept his word,

2.29 aber der arme Goldschmied mußte sein Lebtag die beiden Höcker tragen und seinen kahlen Kopf mit einer Mütze bedecken.

but the poor goldsmith had to wear the two humps for the rest of his life and cover his bald head with a cap.

Der Riese und der Schneider

The Giant and the Tailor

1.1 Einem Schneider, der ein großer Prahler war, aber ein schlechter Zahler, kam es in den Sinn, ein wenig auszugehen und sich in dem Walde umzuschauen.
A tailor, who was a great boaster but a bad payer, thought of going out for a while and looking around in the forest.

1.2 Sobald er nur konnte, verließ er seine Werkstatt,
As soon as he could, he left his workshop,

wanderte seinen Weg	wandered his way
über Brücke und Steg,	over bridge and footbridge,
bald da, bald dort,	soon there, soon there,
immer fort und fort.	on and on and on.

Als er nun draußen war, erblickte er in der blauen Ferne einen steilen Berg und dahinter einen himmelhohen Turm, der aus einem wilden und finsteren Walde hervorragte.

3.1

When he was outside, he saw a steep mountain in the blue distance and behind it a sky-high tower rising out of a wild and dark forest.

»Potz Blitz!« rief der Schneider, »was ist das?«

3.2

"What's that?" cried the tailor, "What's that?"

und weil ihn die Neugierde gewaltig stach,

3.3

and because his curiosity got the better of him,

so ging er frisch darauf los.

3.4

he went straight for it.

Was sperrte er aber Maul und Augen auf, als er in die Nähe kam, denn der Turm hatte Beine, sprang in einem Satz über den steilen Berg und stand als ein großmächtiger Riese vor dem Schneider.

3.5

But he opened his mouth and eyes when he came near it, for the tower had legs, leapt over the steep hill in a single bound and stood before the tailor as a mighty giant.

»Was willst du hier, du winziges Fliegenbein.«

3.6

"What do you want here, you tiny fly- leg."

rief der mit einer Stimme, als wenn's von allen Seiten donnerte.

3.7

he shouted in a voice that sounded like thunder from all sides.

Der Schneider wisperte:

3.8

The tailor whispered,

3.9 »Ich will mich umschauen, ob ich mein Stückchen Brot in dem Walde verdienen kann.«

"I want to look around to see if I can earn my bread in the forest."

3.10 »Wenn's um die Zeit ist.« sagte der Riese,

"If it's about that time." said the giant,

3.11 »so kannst du ja bei mir im Dienst eintreten.«

"you can come and work for me."

3.12 »Wenn's sein muß, warum das nicht?

"If I have to, why not?

3.13 Was krieg ich aber für einen Lohn?«

But what wages will I get?"

3.14 »Was du für einen Lohn kriegst?« sagte der Riese,

"What wages do you get?" said the giant,

3.15 »das sollst du hören.

"I'll tell you.

3.16 Jährlich dreihundertundfünfundsechzig Tage, und wenn's ein Schaltjahr ist, noch einen obendrein.

Three hundred and sixty-five days a year, and if it's a leap year, one more on top of that.

3.17 Ist dir das recht?«

Is that all right with you?"

3.18 »Meinetwegen.«

"Fine by me."

3.19 antwortete der Schneider und dachte in seinem Sinn:

replied the tailor, thinking to himself:

»Man muß sich strecken nach seiner Decke.   3.20
"You have to stretch out for your blanket.

Ich suche mich bald wieder loszumachen.«   3.21
I'll try to get rid of it soon."

Darauf sprach der Riese zu ihm: 4.1
Then the giant said to him:

»Geh, kleiner Halunke, und hol mir einen Krug   4.2
Wasser.«
"Go, little rascal, and fetch me a jug of water."

»Warum nicht lieber gleich den Brunnen mitsamt der   4.3
Quelle?«
"Why not the well and the spring instead?"

fragte der Prahlhans und ging mit dem Krug zu dem   4.4
Wasser.
asked the braggart and went to the water with the jug.

»Was? den Brunnen mitsamt der Quelle?«   4.5
"What? The well and the spring?"

brummte der Riese, der ein bißchen tölpisch und   4.6
albern war, in den Bart hinein und fing an sich zu
fürchten,
grumbled the giant, who was a little foolish and silly, into
his beard, and began to be afraid,

»der Kerl kann mehr als Äpfel braten;   4.7
"that fellow can do more than roast apples;

der hat einen Alraun im Leib.   4.8
he has a mandrake in his body.

4.9 Sei auf deiner Hut, alter Hans, das ist kein Diener für
dich.«

Be on your guard, old Hans, this is no servant for you."

4.10 Als der Schneider das Wasser gebracht hatte, befahl
ihm der Riese, in dem Walde ein paar Scheite Holz zu
hauen und heimzutragen.

When the tailor had brought the water, the giant ordered
him to cut a few logs of wood in the forest and carry them
home.

4.11 »Warum nicht lieber den ganzen Wald mit einem
Streich,

"Why not the whole forest in one fell swoop,

den ganzen Wald	the whole forest
mit jung und alt,	with young and old,
mit allem, was er hat,	with everything he has,
knorzig und glatt?«	gnarled and smooth?"

6.1 fragte das Schneiderlein, und ging das Holz zu hauen.
»Was?

asked the little tailor, and went to hew the wood. "What?

den ganzen Wald	the whole forest
mit jung und alt,	with young and old,
mit allem, was er hat,	with everything he has,
knorzig und glatt?	gnarled and smooth?

und den Brunnen mitsamt der Quelle?« 8.1

and the well and the spring?"

brummte der leichtgläubige Riese in den Bart und 8.2
fürchtete sich noch mehr,

the gullible giant grumbled into his beard, even more
frightened,

»der Kerl kann mehr als Äpfel braten; 8.3

"that fellow can do more than roast apples;

der hat einen Alraun im Leib. 8.4

he has a mandrake in his body.

Sei auf deiner Hut, alter Hans, das ist kein Diener für 8.5
dich.«

Be on your guard, old Hans, this is no servant for you."

Wie der Schneider das Holz gebracht hatte, befahl 8.6
ihm der Riese, zwei oder drei wilde Schweine zum
Abendessen zu schießen.

When the tailor had brought the wood, the giant ordered
him to shoot two or three wild pigs for dinner.

»Warum nicht lieber gleich tausend auf einen Schuß 8.7
und die alle hierher?«

"Why not a thousand at one shot and bring them all here?"

fragte der hoffärtige Schneider. »Was?« 8.8

asked the arrogant tailor. "What?"

rief der Hasenfuß von einem Riesen und war heftig 8.9
erschrocken,

cried the hare's foot of a giant, startled,

»laß es nur für heute gut sein und lege dich schlafen.« 8.10

"just leave it alone for today and go to bed."

102

9.1 Der Riese fürchtete sich so gewaltig, daß er die ganze Nacht kein Auge zuthun konnte und hin und her dachte, wie er's anfangen sollte, um sich den verwünschten Hexenmeister von Diener je eher je lieber vom Hals zu schaffen.

The giant was so terrified that he couldn't sleep a wink all night and thought back and forth about how he should go about getting rid of the cursed sorcerer of servants the sooner the better.

9.2 Kommt Zeit, kommt Rat.

Come time, come advice.

9.3 Am anderen Morgen gingen der Riese und der Schneider zu einem Sumpf,

The next morning,

9.4 um den ringsherum eine Menge Weidenbäume standen.

the giant and the tailor went to a swamp surrounded by a lot of willow trees.

9.5 Da sprach der Riese: »Hör einmal.

Then the giant said, "Listen.

9.6 Schneider, setz dich auf eine von den Weidenruten, ich möchte um mein Leben gern sehen, ob du imstande bist sie herabzubiegen.«

Tailor, sit on one of the willow rods, I would like to see for the life of me if you are able to bend it down."

9.7 Husch, saß das Schneiderlein oben, hielt den Atem ein und machte sich schwer, so schwer, daß sich die Gerte niederbog.

Shoo, the little tailor sat up, held his breath and made himself heavy, so heavy that the whip bent down.

Als er aber wieder Atem schöpfen mußte, da
schnellte sie ihn, weil er zum Unglück kein
Bügeleisen in die Tasche gesteckt hatte, zu großer
Freude des Riesen so weit in die Höhe, daß man ihn
gar nicht mehr sehen konnte.

9.8

But when he had to catch his breath again, because,
unfortunately, he had not put an iron in his pocket, the
whip flew up so high that he could no longer be seen, much
to the giant's delight.

Wenn er nicht wieder heruntergefallen ist,

9.9

If he didn't fall down again,

so wird er wohl noch oben in der Luft
herumschweben.

9.10

he will probably still be floating around in the air.

Der Nagel

The Nail

1.1 Ein Kaufmann hatte auf der Messe gute Geschäfte gemacht,

A merchant had done good business at the fair,

1.2 alle Waaren verkauft und seine Geldkatze mit Gold und Silber gespickt.

sold all his goods and larded his wallet with gold and silver.

1.3 Er wollte jetzt heimreisen und vor Einbruch der Nacht zu Hause sein.

He now wanted to travel home and be back before nightfall.

1.4 Er packte also den Mantelsack mit dem Geld auf sein Pferd und ritt fort.

So he packed the sack with the money on his horse and rode off.

1.5 Zu Mittag rastete er in einer Stadt;

At midday he stopped in a town;

1.6 als er weiter wollte, führte ihm der Hausknecht das Roß vor, sprach aber:

when he wanted to continue, the servant showed him the horse, but said:

»Herr,   1.7
"Sir,

am linken Hinterfuß fehlt im Hufeisen ein Nagel.«   1.8
a nail is missing from the horseshoe on the left hind foot."

»Laß ihn fehlen.« erwiderte der Kaufmann,   1.9
"Let it be missing." replied the merchant,

»die sechs Stunden, die ich noch zu machen habe,   1.10
wird das Eisen wohl festhalten.
"the iron will probably hold for the six hours I still
have to do.

Ich habe Eile.«   1.11
I'm in a hurry."

Nachmittags als er wieder abgestiegen war und dem 1.12
Roß Brot geben ließ, kam der Knecht in die Stube und
sagte:
In the afternoon, when he had dismounted again and had
the horse given bread, the servant came into the parlor and
said,

»Herr. Eurem Pferde fehlt am linken Hinterfuß ein 1.13
Hufeisen.
"Sir. Your horse is missing a shoe on its left hind foot.

Soll ich's zum Schmied führen?«   1.14
Shall I take it to the blacksmith?"

»Laß es fehlen.« erwiderte der Herr,   1.15
"Leave it alone." replied the master,

»die paar Stunden, die noch übrig sind, wird das   1.16
Pferd wohl aushalten.
"the horse will probably last the few hours that are left.

1.17 **Ich habe Eile.«**

I'm in a hurry."

1.18 **Er ritt fort, aber nicht lange, so fing das Pferd zu hinken an.**

He rode off, but not for long, and the horse began to limp.

1.19 **Es hinkte nicht lange, so fing es an zu stolpern, und es stolperte nicht lange, so fiel es nieder und brach ein Bein.**

Before long, it began to stumble, and before long, it fell down and broke a leg.

1.20 **Der Kaufmann mußte das Pferd liegen lassen, den Mantelsack abschnallen, auf die Schulter nehmen und zu Fuß nach Hause, gehen, wo er erst spät in der Nacht anlangte.**

The merchant had to leave the horse, unbuckle his coat sack, put it on his shoulder and walk home, where he arrived late at night.

1.21 **»An allem Unglück.« sprach er zu sich selbst,**

"All the bad luck." he said to himself,

1.22 **»ist der verwünschte Nagel schuld.« Eile mit Weile.**

"is the fault of the cursed nail." Haste makes waste.

Der arme Junge im Grabe

The Poor Boy in the Grave

1.1 Es war einmal ein armer Hirtenjunge, dem war Vater
und Mutter gestorben, und er war von der Obrigkeit
einem reichen Mann in das Haus gegeben, der sollte
ihn ernähren und erziehen.

Once upon a time there was a poor shepherd boy whose
father and mother had died, and he was given by the
authorities into the home of a rich man who was to feed
and educate him.

1.2 Der Mann aber und seine Frau hatten ein böses Herz,
waren bei allem Reichtum geizig und mißgünstig,
und ärgerten sich, wenn jemand einen Bissen von
ihrem Brot in den Mund steckte.

But the man and his wife had wicked hearts, were stingy
and resentful despite their wealth, and were angry if
anyone put a morsel of their bread in their mouths.

1.3 Der arme Junge mochte thun was er wollte, er erhielt
wenig zu essen, aber desto mehr Schläge.

The poor boy could do what he liked, he received little to
eat, but all the more beatings.

Eines Tages sollte er die Glucke mit ihren Küchlein hüten. 2.1

One day he was supposed to look after the mother hen and her chicks.

Sie verlief sich aber mit ihren Jungen durch einen Heckenzaun; 2.2

But she got lost with her chicks through a hedge fence;

gleich schoß der Habicht herab und entführte sie durch die Lüfte. 2.3

immediately the hawk swooped down and snatched them away through the air.

Der Junge schrie aus Leibeskräften: 2.4

The boy screamed at the top of his lungs:

»Dieb, Dieb, Spitzbub.« Aber was half das? 2.5

"Thief, thief, rogue." But what good was that?

Der Habicht brachte seinen Raub nicht wieder zurück. 2.6

The hawk did not bring back his robbery.

Der Mann hörte den Lärm, lief herbei, und als er vernahm, daß seine Henne weg war, so geriet er in Wut und gab dem Jungen eine solche Tracht Schläge, daß er sich ein paar Tage lang nicht regen konnte. 2.7

The man heard the noise, ran over, and when he heard that his hen was gone, he flew into a rage and gave the boy such a beating that he could not move for a few days.

Nun mußte er die Küchlein ohne die Henne hüten, aber da war die Not noch größer, das eine lief dahin, das andere dorthin. 2.8

Now he had to look after the little chicks without the hen, but then the trouble was even greater, one ran there and the other there.

2.9 Da meinte er es klug zu machen, wenn er sie alle zusammen an eine Schnur bände, weil ihm dann der Habicht keins wegstehlen könnte.

So he thought he would be wise if he tied them all together on a string, because then the hawk would not be able to steal one away from him.

2.10 Aber weit gefehlt.

But far from it.

2.11 Nach ein paar Tagen, als er von dem Herumlaufen und vom Hunger ermüdet einschlief, kam der Raubvogel und packte eins von den Küchlein, und da die anderen daran festhingen, so trug er sie alle mit fort, setzte sich auf einen Baum und schluckte sie hinunter.

After a few days, when he fell asleep, tired of running around and hungry, the bird of prey came and grabbed one of the chicks, and as the others were hanging on to it, it carried them all away, sat down in a tree and swallowed them.

2.12 Der Bauer kam eben nach Hause, und als er das Unglück sah, erboste er sich und schlug den Jungen so unbarmherzig, daß er mehrere Tage im Bette liegen mußte.

The farmer came home just then, and when he saw the misfortune, he was furious, and beat the boy so unmercifully that he had to lie in bed for several days.

3.1 Als er wieder auf den Beinen war, sprach der Bauer zu ihm:

When he was on his feet again, the farmer said to him:

»Du bist mir zu dumm, ich kann dich zum Hüten, 3.2
nicht brauchen, du sollst als Bote gehen.«

"You are too stupid for me, I can't use you for herding, you
should go as a messenger."

Da schickte er ihn zum Richter, dem er einen Korb 3.3
voll Trauben bringen sollte, und gab ihm noch einen
Brief mit.

So he sent him to the judge, to whom he was to bring a
basket of grapes, and gave him a letter to take with him.

Unterwegs plagte Hunger und Durst den armen 3.4
Jungen so heftig, daß er zwei von den Trauben aß.

On the way the poor boy was so hungry and thirsty that he
ate two of the grapes.

Er brachte dem. 3.5

He brought the basket to the judge.

Richter den Korb; als dieser aber den Brief gelesen 3.6
und die Trauben gezählt hatte, so sagte er,

But when the judge had read the letter and counted the
grapes, he said,

»Es fehlen zwei Stück.« 3.7

"There are two grapes missing."

Der Junge gestand ganz ehrlich, daß er, von Hunger 3.8
und Durst getrieben, die fehlenden verzehrt habe.

The boy confessed quite honestly that, driven by hunger
and thirst, he had eaten the missing ones.

Der Richter schrieb einen Brief an den Bauer und 3.9
verlangte noch einmal so viel Trauben.

The judge wrote a letter to the farmer and asked for the
same number of grapes again.

3.10 **Auch diese mußte der Junge mit einem Brief hintragen.**

The boy also had to carry these with a letter.

3.11 **Als ihn wieder so gewaltig hungerte und durstete, so konnte er sich nicht anders helfen, er verzehrte abermals zwei Trauben.**

When he was so hungry and thirsty again, he could not help himself and ate two more grapes.

3.12 **Doch nahm er vorher den Brief aus dem Korb, legte ihn unter einen Stein und setzte sich darauf, damit der Brief nicht zusehen und ihn; verraten könnte.**

But first he took the letter out of the basket, put it under a stone and sat down on it, so that the letter might not be seen and betray him.

3.13 **Der Richter aber stellte ihn doch der fehlenden Stücke wegen zur Rede.**

But the judge confronted him about the missing pieces.

3.14 **»Ach.« sagte der Junge, »wie habt Ihr das erfahren?**

"Oh." said the boy, "how did you find out?

3.15 **Der Brief konnte es nicht wissen,**

The letter could not have known,

3.16 **denn ich hatte ihn zuvor unter einen Stein gelegt.«**

for I had put it under a stone beforehand."

Der Richter mußte über die Einfalt lachen und schickte, dem Mann einen Brief, worin er ihn ermahnte, den armen Jungen besser zu halten und es ihm an Speise und Trank nicht fehlen zu lassen; auch möchte er ihn lehren was Recht und Unrecht sei.

3.17

The judge laughed at his simplicity, and sent a letter to the man, in which he exhorted him to keep the poor boy better, and not to let him want for food and drink, and to teach him what was right and wrong.

»Ich will dir den Unterschied schon zeigen.«

4.1

"I will show you the difference."

sagte der harte Mann;

4.2

said the hard man;

»willst du aber essen, so mußt du auch arbeiten, und thust du etwas Unrechtes, so sollst du durch Schläge hinlänglich belehrt werden.«

4.3

"but if you want to eat, you must also work, and if you do something wrong, you shall be sufficiently instructed by blows."

Am folgenden Tage stellte er ihn an eine schwere Arbeit.

4.4

The next day he set him to hard labor.

Er sollte ein paar Bund Stroh zum Futter für die Pferde schneiden; dabei drohte der Mann:

4.5

He was to cut a few bundles of straw to feed the horses, and the man threatened:

»In fünf Stunden.« sprach er,

4.6

"I'll be back in five hours." he said,

4.7 »bin ich wieder zurück, wenn dann das Stroh nicht zu Häcksel geschnitten ist, so schlage ich dich so lange, bis du kein Glied mehr regen kannst.«

"and if the straw is not cut into chaff, I'll beat you until you can't move a limb."

4.8 Der Bauer ging mit seiner Frau, dem Knecht und der Magd auf den Jahrmarkt und ließ dem Jungen nichts zurück als ein kleines Stück Brot.

The farmer went to the fair with his wife, the farmhand and the maid, leaving the boy with nothing but a small piece of bread.

4.9 Der Junge stellte sich an den Strohstuhl und fing an aus allen Leibeskräften zu arbeiten.

The boy stood at the straw chair and began to work with all his might.

4.10 Da ihm dabei, heiß ward, so zog er sein Röcklein aus und warf's auf das Stroh.

As he was getting hot, he took off his skirt and threw it on the straw.

4.11 Inder Angst, nicht fertig zu werden, schnitt er immer zu, und in seinem Eifer zerschnitt er unvermerkt mit dem Stroh auch sein Röcklein.

Fearing that he would not finish, he kept cutting, and in his zeal he cut his skirt along with the straw.

4.12 Zu spät ward er das Unglück gewahr, das sich nicht wieder gut machen ließ.

Too late he realized the misfortune that could not be repaired.

4.13 »Ach.« rief er, »jetzt ist es aus mit mir.

"Alas." he cried, "now I'm finished.

Der böse Mann hat mir nicht umsonst gedroht, 4.14
kommt er zurück und sieht, was ich gethan habe,
so schlägt er mich tot.
The wicked man has not threatened me in vain; if he comes
back and sees what I have done, he will beat me to death.

Lieber will ich mir selbst das Leben nehmen.« 4.15
I'd rather take my own life."

Der Junge hatte einmal gehört wie die Bäuerin 5.1
sprach:
The boy had once heard the farmer's wife say:

»Unter dem Bett habe ich einen Topf mit Gift stehen.« 5.2
"I have a pot of poison under the bed."

Sie hatte es aber nur gesagt, um die Näscher 5.3
zurückzuhalten, denn es war Honig darin.
But she had only said it to keep the nibblers back, because
there was honey in it.

Der Junge kroch unter das Bett, 5.4
The boy crawled under the bed,

holte den Topf hervor und aß ihn ganz aus. 5.5
took out the pot and ate it all.

»Ich weiß nicht.« sprach er, 5.6
"I don't know." he said,

»die Leute sagen, der Tod sei bitter, mir schmeckt er 5.7
süß.
"people say death is bitter, but it tastes sweet to me.

Kein Wunder, daß die Bäuerin sich so oft den Tod 5.8
wünscht.«
No wonder the farmer's wife so often wishes for death."

5.9 Er setzte sich auf ein Stühlchen und war gefaßt zu sterben.

He sat down on a little chair and was ready to die.

5.10 Aber statt daß er schwächer werden sollte,

But instead of becoming weaker,

5.11 fühlte er sich von der nahrhaften Speise gestärkt.

he felt invigorated by the nourishing food.

5.12 »Es muß kein Gift gewesen sein.« sagte er,

"It must not have been poison." he said,

5.13 »aber der Bauer hat einmal gesagt in seinem Kleiderkasten läge ein Fläschchen mit Fliegengift, das wird wohl das wahre Gift sein und mir den Tod bringen.«

"but the farmer once said that there was a bottle of fly poison in his wardrobe; that will probably be the real poison and bring me death."

5.14 Es war aber kein Fliegengift, sondern Ungarwein.

But it wasn't fly poison, it was Hungarian wine.

5.15 Der Junge holte die Flasche heraus und trank sie aus.

The boy took out the bottle and drank it.

5.16 »Auch dieser Tod schmeckt süß.«

"Even this death tastes sweet."

5.17 sagte er, doch als bald hernach der Wein anfing, ihm ins Gehirn zu steigen und ihn zu betäuben, so meinte er, sein Ende nahte heran.

he said, but when soon afterward the wine began to get into his brain and numb him, he thought his end was near.

»Ich fühle, daß ich sterben muß.« sprach er,

"I feel that I must die." he said,

5.18

»ich will hinaus auf den Kirchhof gehen und ein Grab suchen.«

"I will go out into the churchyard and look for a grave."

5.19

Er taumelte fort,

He staggered away,

5.20

erreichte den Kirchhof und legte sich in ein frisch geöffnetes Grab.

reached the churchyard and lay down in a freshly opened grave.

5.21

Die Sinne verschwanden ihm immer mehr.

His senses began to fade.

5.22

In der Nähe stand ein Wirtshaus, wo eine Hochzeit gefeiert wurde;

Nearby was an inn where a wedding was being celebrated;

5.23

als er die Musik hörte, deuchte er sich schon im Paradies zu sein, bis er endlich alle Besinnung verlor.

when he heard the music, he thought he was already in paradise, until he finally lost all consciousness.

5.24

Der arme Junge erwachte nicht wieder:

The poor boy never woke up again:

5.25

die Glut des heißen Weines und der kalte Tau der Nacht nahmen ihm das Leben, und er verblieb in dem Grabe, in das er sich selbst gelegt hatte.

the heat of the hot wine and the cold dew of the night took his life, and he remained in the grave in which he had laid himself.

5.26

6.1 **Als der Bauer die Nachricht von dem Tode des Jungen erhielt, erschrak er und fürchtete vor das Gericht geführt zu werden, ja die Angst faßte ihn so gewaltig, daß er ohnmächtig zur Erde sank.**

When the farmer received the news of the boy's death, he was frightened and feared to be brought before the court, indeed his fear gripped him so violently that he sank to the ground in a faint.

6.2 **Die Frau, die mit einer Pfanne voll Schmalz am Herde stand, lief herzu, um ihm Beistand zu leisten.**

The woman, who was standing by the hearth with a pan of lard, ran over to succor him.

6.3 **Aber das Feuer schlug in die Pfanne,**

But the fire caught the pan,

6.4 **ergriff das ganze Haus und nach wenigen Stunden lag es schon in Asche.**

engulfed the whole house and after a few hours it lay in ashes.

6.5 **Die Jahre, die sie noch zu leben hatten, brachten sie, von Gewissensbissen geplagt, in Armut und Elend zu.**

They spent the years they had left to live in poverty and misery, plagued by remorse.

Der Froschkönig oder der eiserne Heinrich

The Frog King or the Iron Henry

1.1 In den alten Zeiten, wo das Wünschen noch geholfen hat, lebte ein König, dessen Töchter waren alle schön, aber die jüngste war so schön, daß die Sonne selber, die doch so vieles gesehen hat, sich verwunderte, so oft sie ihr ins Gesicht schien.

In the old days, when wishing still helped, there lived a king whose daughters were all beautiful, but the youngest was so beautiful that the sun itself, which had seen so many things, was astonished when it often shone in her face.

1.2 Nahe bei dem Schlosse des Königs lag ein großer dunkler Wald,

Near the king's castle was a large dark wood,

1.3 und in dem Walde unter einer alten Linde war ein Brunnen;

and in the wood under an old lime-tree was a well;

wenn nun der Tag sehr heiß war, so ging das   1.4
Königskind hinaus in den Wald und setzte sich
an den Rand des kühlen Brunnens, und wenn sie
Langeweile hatte, so nahm sie eine goldene Kugel,
warf sie in die Höhe und fing sie wieder;

and when the day was very hot, the king's child went out
into the wood and sat down on the edge of the cool well,
and when she was bored she took a golden ball, threw it up
into the air, and caught it again;

und das war ihr liebstes Spielwerk.   1.5

and that was her favorite plaything.

Nun trug es sich einmal zu, daß die goldene Kugel der   2.1
Königstochter nicht in ihr Händchen fiel, das sie in
die Höhe gehalten hatte, sondern vorbei auf die Erde
schlug und geradezu ins Wasser hineinrollte.

Now it once happened that the golden ball did not fall
into the little hand of the King's daughter, which she had
held aloft, but struck the earth and rolled straight into the
water.

Die Königstochter folgte ihr mit den Augen nach,   2.2
aber die Kugel verschwand, und der Brunnen war tief,
so tief, daß man keinen Grund sah.

The King's daughter followed it with her eyes, but the ball
disappeared, and the well was deep, so deep that no bottom
could be seen.

Da fing sie an zu weinen und weinte immer lauter   2.3
und konnte sich gar nicht trösten.

Then she began to weep, and wept louder and louder, and
could not comfort herself at all.

Und wie sie so klagte, rief ihr jemand zu: 2.4

And as she wept, someone called out to her,

2.5 »Was hast du vor, Königstochter, du schreist ja, daß sich ein Stein erbarmen möchte.«
"What are you up to, princess, you are crying out for a stone to have mercy on you."

2.6 Sie sah sich um, woher die Stimme käme, da erblickte sie einen Frosch, der seinen dicken häßlichen Kopf aus dem Wasser streckte.
She looked around to see where the voice was coming from, and then she saw a frog sticking its fat, ugly head out of the water.

2.7 »Ach, du bist's, alter Wasserpatscher.« sagte sie,
"Oh, it's you, old water-frog." she said,

2.8 »ich weine über meine goldene Kugel,
"I'm crying over my golden ball,

2.9 die mir in den Brunnen hinabgefallen ist.«
which has fallen into the well."

2.10 »Sei still und weine nicht.« antwortete der Frosch,
"Be quiet and don't cry." replied the frog,

2.11 »ich kann wohl Rat schaffen, aber was giebst du mir, wenn ich dein Spielwerk wieder heraushole?«
"I can give you advice, but what will you give me if I get your toy out again?"

2.12 »Was du haben willst, lieber Frosch.« sagte sie,
"What you want, dear frog." she said,

2.13 »meine Kleider, meine Perlen und Edelsteine, auch noch die goldene Krone, die ich trage.«
"my clothes, my pearls and precious stones, and the golden crown I'm wearing."

Der Frosch antwortete: 2.14
The frog replied,

»Deine Kleider, deine Perlen und Edelsteine, und 2.15
deine goldene Krone, die mag ich nicht;
"Your clothes, your pearls and precious stones, and your
golden crown, I don't like them;

aber wenn du mich lieb haben willst und ich soll dein 2.16
Geselle und Spielkamerad sein, an deinem Tischlein
neben dir sitzen, von deinem goldenen Tellerlein
essen, aus deinem Becherlein trinken, in deinem
Bettlein schlafen:
but if you will love me and I shall be your companion and
playmate, sit at your little table beside you, eat from your
little golden plate, drink from your little cup, sleep in your
little bed:

wenn du mir das versprichst, 2.17
if you promise me that,

so will ich hinuntersteigen und dir die goldene Kugel 2.18
wieder herausholen.«
I will go down and fetch you the golden ball again."

»Ach ja.« sagte sie, 2.19
"Oh yes." she said,

»ich verspreche dir alles, was du willst, wenn du mir 2.20
nur die Kugel wieder bringst.«
"I promise you anything you want, if only you bring me
back the ball."

Sie dachte aber: 2.21
But she thought,

2.22 »Was der einfältige Frosch schwätzt, der sitzt im Wasser bei seinesgleichen und quakt, und kann keines Menschen Geselle sein.«

"What the simple-minded frog talks about, he sits in the water with his own kind and croaks, and cannot be anyone's companion."

3.1 Der Frosch, als er die Zusage erhalten hatte, tauchte seinen Kopf unter, sank hinab und über ein Weilchen kam er wieder heraufgerudert;

The frog, when he had received the promise, plunged his head under water, sank down, and after a little while he came up again;

3.2 hatte die Kugel im Maul und warf sie ins Gras.

he had the ball in his mouth and threw it into the grass.

3.3 Die Königstochter war voll Freude, als sie ihr schönes Spielwerk wieder erblickte, hob es auf und sprang damit fort.

The king's daughter was full of joy when she saw her beautiful toy again, picked it up and jumped away with it.

3.4 »Warte, warte.« rief der Frosch, »nimm mich mit,

"Wait, wait." cried the frog, "take me with you,

3.5 ich kann nicht so laufen wie du.«

I can't walk like you."

3.6 Aber was half ihm, daß er ihr sein quak quak so laut nachschrie als er konnte;

But it didn't help that he shouted his quack quack after her as loud as he could;

sie hörte nicht darauf, eilte nach Haus und hatte bald
den armen Frosch vergessen, der wieder in seinen
Brunnen hinabsteigen mußte.

3.7

she didn't listen, hurried home and soon forgot the poor
frog, who had to go down into his well again.

Am anderen Tage, als sie mit dem König und allen
Hofleuten sich zur Tafel gesetzt hatte und von
ihrem goldenen Tellerlein aß, da kam, plitsch
platsch, plitsch platsch, etwas die Marmortreppe
heraufgekrochen, und als es oben angelangt war,
klopfte es an der Thür und rief:

4.1

The next day, when she had seated herself at table with the
King and all the courtiers, and was eating from her little
golden plate, there came, plop, plop, plop, something crept
up the marble staircase, and when it had reached the top, it
knocked at the door and cried:

»Königstochter, jüngste, mach mir auf.«

4.2

"King's daughter, youngest, open the door for me."

Sie lief und wollte sehen wer draußen wäre, als sie
aber aufmachte, so saß der Frosch davor.

4.3

She ran and wanted to see who was outside, but when she
opened the door, the frog was sitting in front of it.

Da warf sie die Thür hastig zu, setzte sich wieder an
den Tisch, und war ihr ganz angst.

4.4

Then she hastily threw the door shut, sat down again at the
table, and was quite frightened.

Der König sah wohl, daß ihr das Herz gewaltig
klopfte und sprach:

4.5

The King saw that her heart was beating violently, and said,

126

4.6 »Mein Kind, was fürchtest du dich, steht etwa ein Riese vor der Thür und will dich holen?«

"My child, what are you afraid of, is there a giant at the door to take you away?"

4.7 »Ach nein.« antwortete sie, »es ist kein Riese,

"Oh no." she answered, "it is not a giant,

4.8 sondern ein garstiger Frosch.«

but a nasty frog."

4.9 »Was will der Frosch von dir?«

"What does the frog want with you?"

4.10 »Ach lieber Vater, als ich gestern im Walde bei dem Brunnen saß und spielte, da fiel meine goldene Kugel ins Wasser.

"Oh, dear father, yesterday I was sitting in the forest by the well playing and my golden ball fell into the water.

4.11 Und weil ich so weinte, hat sie der Frosch wieder heraufgeholt, und weil er es durchaus verlangte, so versprach ich ihm, er sollte mein Geselle werden, ich dachte aber nimmermehr, daß er aus seinem Wasser heraus könnte.

And because I was crying so much, the frog brought it up again, and because he really wanted it, I promised him that he should become my companion, but I never thought that he could get out of his water.

4.12 Nun ist er draußen und will zu mir herein.«

Now he is outside and wants to come in to me."

4.13 Indem klopfte es zum zweitenmal und rief:

Then he knocked a second time and called out:

»Königstochter, jüngste,

"King's daughter, youngest,

mach mir auf,

open for me,

weißt du nicht, was gestern

don't you know what happened yesterday

du zu mir gesagt

you said to me

bei dem kühlen Brunnenwasser?

with the cool well water?

Königstochter, jüngste,

King's daughter, youngest,

mach mir auf.«

Open up for me."

Da sagte der König: »Was du versprochen hast,   6.1
Then the king said: "What you have promised,

das mußt du auch halten; geh nur und mach ihm auf.«   6.2
you must keep; go and open the door for him."

Sie ging und öffnete die Thür, da hüpfte der Frosch   6.3
herein, ihr immer auf dem Fuße nach, bis zu ihrem
Stuhl.
She went and opened the door, and the frog hopped in,
always following her, up to her chair.

Da saß er und rief: »Heb mich herauf zu dir.«   6.4
There he sat and cried: "Lift me up to you."

Sie zauderte, bis es endlich der König befahl.   6.5
She hesitated until the king finally ordered her to do so.

6.6 Als der Frosch erst auf dem Stuhl war, wollte er auf den Tisch, und als er da saß, sprach er:
Once the frog was on the chair, he wanted to go to the table, and as he sat there he said,

6.7 »Nun schieb mir dein goldenes Tellerlein näher, damit wir zusammen essen.«
"Now push your little golden plate closer to me so that we can eat together."

6.8 Das that sie zwar, aber man sah wohl, daß sie's nicht gerne that.
She did so, but you could see that she did not like it.

6.9 Der Frosch ließ sich's gut schmecken,
The frog enjoyed it very much,

6.10 aber ihr blieb fast jedes Bißlein im Halse.
but almost every morsel remained in her throat.

6.11 Endlich sprach er:
At last he said,

6.12 »Ich habe mich satt gegessen, und bin müde, nun trag mich in dein Kämmerlein und mach dein seiden Bettlein zurecht, da wollen wir uns schlafen legen.«
"I have eaten my fill, and am tired; now carry me into your little chamber, and make up your silken bed, and there we will lie down to sleep."

6.13 Die Königstochter fing an zu weinen und fürchtete sich vor dem kalten Frosch, den sie sich nicht anzurühren getraute, und der nun in ihrem schönen reinen Bettlein schlafen sollte.
The king's daughter began to weep and was afraid of the cold frog, which she dared not touch, and which was now to sleep in her beautiful, clean bed.

Der König aber ward zornig und sprach: 6.14
But the king was angry and said,

»Wer dir geholfen hat, als du in der Not warst, den 6.15
sollst du hernach nicht verachten.«
"Whoever helped you when you were in trouble, you must
not despise him afterward."

Da packte sie ihn mit zwei Fingern, 6.16
So she seized him with two fingers,

trug ihn hinauf und setzte ihn in eine Ecke. 6.17
carried him up and put him in a corner.

Als sie aber im Bette lag, kam er gekrochen und 6.18
sprach:
But as she lay in bed, he crawled up and said:

»Ich bin müde, ich will schlafen so gut wie du; 6.19
"I am tired, I want to sleep as well as you do;

heb mich herauf, oder ich sag's deinem Vater.« 6.20
lift me up, or I will tell your father."

Da ward sie erst bitterböse, 6.21
Then she got bitterly angry,

holte ihn herauf und warf ihn aus allen Kräften wider 6.22
die Wand:
picked him up and threw him against the wall with all her
might:

»Nun wirst du Ruhe haben, du garstiger Frosch.« 6.23
"Now you will have rest, you nasty frog."

7.1 Als er aber herab fiel, war er kein Frosch, sondern ein Königssohn mit schönen freundlichen Augen.

But when he fell down, he was not a frog, but a king's son with beautiful, kind eyes.

7.2 Der war nun nach ihres Vaters Willen ihr lieber Geselle und Gemahl.

He was now her father's favorite companion and husband.

7.3 Da erzählte er ihr, er wäre von einer bösen Hexe verwünscht worden, und niemand hätte ihn aus dem Brunnen erlösen können als sie allein, und morgen wollten sie zusammen in sein Reich gehen.

Then he told her that he had been cursed by a wicked witch, and that no one could have rescued him from the well but she alone, and that tomorrow they would go to his kingdom together.

7.4 Dann schliefen sie ein, und am anderen Morgen, als die Sonne sie aufweckte, kam ein Wagen herangefahren mit acht weißen Pferden bespannt, die hatten weiße Straußfedern auf dem Kopf, und gingen in goldenen Ketten, und hinten stand der Diener des jungen Königs, das war der treue Heinrich.

Then they fell asleep, and the next morning, when the sun woke them up, a carriage came driving up with eight white horses, with white ostrich feathers on their heads, and walking in golden chains, and behind them stood the young king's servant, that was faithful Henry.

7.5 Der treue Heinrich hatte sich so betrübt, als sein Herr war in einen Frosch verwandelt worden, daß er drei eiserne Bande hatte um sein Herz legen lassen, damit es ihm nicht vor Weh und Traurigkeit zerspränge.

Faithful Henry had been so sad when his master had been turned into a frog, that he had three iron bands put round his heart, that it might not burst with pain and sorrow.

Der Wagen aber sollte den jungen König in sein Reich abholen; 7.6
But the carriage was to fetch the young king to his kingdom;

der treue Heinrich hob beide hinein, stellte sich wieder hinten auf und war voller Freude über die Erlösung. 7.7
faithful Henry lifted them both into it, stood in the back again, and was full of joy at his deliverance.

Und als sie ein Stück Weges gefahren waren, hörte der Königssohn, daß es hinter ihm krachte, als wäre etwas zerbrochen. 7.8
And when they had gone some distance, the king's son heard a crash behind him, as if something had broken.

Da drehte er sich um und rief: 7.9
Then he turned around and called out:

»Heinrich, der Wagen bricht.«

"Heinrich, the car is breaking."

»Nein, Herr, der Wagen nicht,

"No, sir, not the car,

es ist ein Band von meinem Herzen,

it is a ribbon from my heart,

das da lag in großen Schmerzen,

that lay there in great pain,

als ihr in dem Brunnen saßt,

when you were sitting in the well,

als ihr eine Fretsche (Frosch) wast (wart).«

when you were a frog."

132

9.1 Doch einmal und noch einmal krachte es auf dem Wege, und der Königssohn meinte immer, der Wagen bräche, und es waren doch nur die Bande, die vom Herzen des treuen Heinrich absprangen, weil sein Herr erlöst und glücklich war.

But once and again there was a crash on the way, and the king's son always thought the carriage would break, and yet it was only the bonds that broke from faithful Henry's heart because his master was redeemed and happy.

Die wahre Braut

The True Bride

1.1 Es war einmal ein Mädchen, das war jung und schön, aber seine Mutter war ihm früh gestorben und die Stiefmutter that ihm alles gebrannte Herzeleid an.

Once upon a time there was a girl who was young and beautiful, but her mother had died early and her stepmother did everything she could to make her heart ache.

1.2 Wenn sie ihm eine Arbeit auftrug, sie mochte noch so schwer sein, so ging es unverdrossen daran und that was in seinen Kräften stand.

When she gave her a job to do, however hard it might be, she went at it undaunted and did what she could.

1.3 Aber es konnte damit das Herz der bösen Frau nicht rühren, immer war sie unzufrieden, immer war es nicht genug.

But he could not stir the heart of the wicked woman, she was always dissatisfied, always not enough.

Je fleißiger es arbeitete, je mehr ward ihm aufgelegt, und sie hatte keinen anderen Gedanken, als wie sie ihm eine größere Last aufbürden und das Leben recht sauer machen wollte.

1.4

The harder she worked, the more was laid upon her, and she had no other thought than how she could make her life more burdensome and sour.

Eines Tages sagte sie zu ihm:

2.1

One day she said to him:

»Da hast du zwölf Pfund Federn, die sollst du abschleißen, und wenn du nicht heute abend damit fertig bist, so wartet eine Tracht Schläge auf dich.

2.2

"You've got twelve pounds of feathers to wear out, and if you don't finish them tonight, you'll get a beating.

Meinst du, du könntest den ganzen Tag faulenzen?«

2.3

Do you think you could laze around all day?"

Das arme Mädchen setzte sich zu der Arbeit nieder, aber die Thränen flossen ihm dabei über die Wangen herab, denn es sah wohl, daß es unmöglich war, mit der Arbeit in einem Tage zu Ende zu kommen.

2.4

The poor girl sat down to her work, but the tears streamed down her cheeks, for she saw that it was impossible to finish the work in one day.

Wenn es ein Häufchen Federn vor sich liegen hatte und es seufzte oder schlug in seiner Angst die Hände zusammen, so stoben sie auseinander und es mußte sie wieder auflesen und von neuem anfangen.

2.5

If she had a heap of feathers lying before her, and she sighed or struck her hands together in her anxiety, they scattered, and she had to pick them up again and begin afresh.

2.6 Da stützte es einmal die Ellbogen auf den Tisch, legte sein Gesicht in beide Hände, und rief:

Then once she leaned her elbows on the table, put her face in both hands, and cried,

2.7 »Ist denn niemand auf Gottes Erdboden, der sich meiner erbarmt?«

"Is there no one on God's earth who will have mercy on me?"

2.8 Indem hörte es eine sanfte Stimme, die sprach:

Then she heard a gentle voice saying:

2.9 »Tröste dich, mein Kind, ich bin gekommen, dir zu helfen.«

"Take comfort, my child, I have come to help you."

2.10 Das Mädchen blickte auf und eine alte Frau stand neben ihm.

The girl looked up and an old woman was standing beside her.

2.11 Sie faßte das Mädchen freundlich an der Hand und sprach,

She took the girl kindly by the hand and said,

2.12 »Vertraue mir nur an was dich drückt.«

"Just confide in me what is troubling you."

2.13 Da sie so herzlich sprach, so erzählte ihr das Mädchen von seinem traurigen Leben, daß ihm eine Last auf die andere gelegt würde und es mit den aufgegebenen Arbeiten nicht mehr zu Ende kommen könnte.

As she spoke so warmly, the girl told her about her sad life, that one burden was being placed on top of another and that she could no longer finish the work she had given up.

»Wenn ich mit diesen Federn heute abend nicht fertig bin,   2.14
"If I am not finished with these feathers this evening,

so schlägt mich die Stiefmutter;   2.15
my stepmother will beat me;

sie hat mir's angedroht, und ich weiß, sie hält Wort.«   2.16
she has threatened to do so, and I know she will keep her word."

Ihre Thränen fingen wieder an zu fließen, aber, die gute Alte sprach: 2.17
Her tears began to flow again, but the good old woman said,

»Sei unbesorgt, mein Kind, ruhe dich aus, ich will derweil deine Arbeit verrichten.«   2.18
"Don't worry, my child, rest, I will do your work in the meantime."

Das Mädchen legte sich auf sein Bett und schlief bald ein.   2.19
The girl lay down on her bed and soon fell asleep.

Die Alte setzte sich an den Tisch zu den Federn, hu!   2.20
The old woman sat down at the table with the feathers, ho!

wie flogen sie von den Kielen ab,   2.21
how they flew off the quills,

die sie mit ihren dürren Händen kaum berührte.   2.22
which she barely touched with her thin hands.

Bald war sie mit den zwölf Pfund fertig.   2.23
Soon she had finished the twelve pounds.

2.24 Als das Mädchen erwachte, lagen große schneeweiße Haufen aufgetürmt, und alles war im Zimmer reinlich aufgeräumt;

When the girl awoke, there were great snow-white heaps piled up, and everything in the room was neat and tidy;

2.25 aber die Alte war verschwunden.

but the old woman had disappeared.

2.26 Das Mädchen dankte Gott und saß still, bis der Abend kam.

The girl thanked God and sat quietly until evening came.

2.27 Da trat die Stiefmutter herein und staunte über die vollbrachte Arbeit.

Then the stepmother came in and marveled at the work she had done.

2.28 »Siehst du, Trulle.« sprach sie,

"You see, Trulle." she said,

2.29 »was man ausrichtet, wenn man fleißig ist?

"what one accomplishes when one is industrious?

2.30 Hättest du nicht noch etwas anderes vornehmen können?

Couldn't you have done something else?

2.31 Aber da sitzest du und legst die Hände in den Schoß.«

But there you sit and put your hands in your lap."

2.32 Als sie hinausging, sprach sie,

As she went out, she said,

2.33 »Die Kreatur kann mehr als Brot essen,

"The creature can eat more than bread,

ich muß ihr schwerere Arbeit auflegen.«   2.34
I must set her heavier work."

Am anderen Morgen rief sie das Mädchen und   3.1
sprach:
The next morning, she called the girl and said,

»Da hast du einen Löffel, damit schöpfe mir den   3.2
großen Teich aus, der bei dem Garten liegt.
"Here's a spoon for you to scoop out the big pond by the
garden.

Und wenn du damit abends nicht zu Rande   3.3
gekommen bist,
And if you don't finish it in the evening,

so weißt du was erfolgt.«   3.4
you know what will happen."

Das Mädchen nahm den Löffel und sah, daß er   3.5
durchlöchert war und wenn er es auch nicht gewesen
wäre, es hätte nimmermehr damit den Teich
ausgeschöpft.
The girl took the spoon and saw that it was full of holes, and
even if it had not been, she would never have scooped out
the pond with it.

Es machte sich gleich an die Arbeit, kniete am   3.6
Wasser, in das seine Thränen fielen, und schöpfte.
She at once set to work, knelt down by the water, into
which her tears fell, and drew.

Aber die gute Alte erschien wieder, und als sie die   3.7
Ursache von seinem Kummer erfuhr, sprach sie:
But the good old woman appeared again, and when she
learned the cause of his sorrow, she said,

3.8 »Sei getrost, mein Kind, geh in das Gebüsch und lege dich schlafen, ich will deine Arbeit schon thun.«
"Be comforted, my child, go into the bushes and lie down to sleep, I will do your work."

3.9 Als die Alte allein war, berührte sie nur den Teich:
When the old woman was alone, she only touched the pond:

3.10 wie ein Dunst stieg das Wasser in die Höhe und vermischte sich mit den Wolken.
the water rose like a mist and mingled with the clouds.

3.11 Allmählich, ward der Teich leer, und als das Mädchen vor Sonnenuntergang erwachte und herbeikam, so sah es nur noch die Fische, die in dem Schlamm zappelten.
Gradually, the pond became empty, and when the girl woke up before sunset and came over, all she could see were the fish wriggling in the mud.

3.12 Es ging zu der Stiefmutter und zeigte ihr an, daß die Arbeit vollbracht wäre.
She went to her stepmother and told her that the work was done.

3.13 »Du hättest längst fertig sein sollen.«
"You should have finished long ago."

3.14 sagte sie und ward blaß: Vor Ärger, aber sie sann etwas Neues aus.
she said, turning pale with anger, but she thought of something new.

4.1 Am dritten Morgen sprach sie zu dem Mädchen:
On the third morning she said to the girl:

»Dort in der. 4.2
"There in the plain you must build me a beautiful castle.

Ebene mußt du mir ein schönes Schloß bauen und 4.3
zum Abend muß es fertig sein.«
You must build me a beautiful castle and it must be finished
by evening."

Das Mädchen erschrak und sagte, 4.4
The girl was frightened and said,

»Wie kann ich ein so großes Werk vollbringen?« 4.5
"How can I accomplish such a great work?"

»Ich dulde keinen Widerspruch.« schrie die 4.6
Stiefmutter,
"I won't tolerate any contradiction." cried the stepmother,

»kannst du mit einem durchlöcherten Löffel einen 4.7
Teich ausschöpfen,
"if you can scoop out a pond with a spoon full of holes,

so kannst du auch ein Schloß bauen. 4.8
you can build a castle too.

Noch heute will ich es beziehen, und wenn etwas 4.9
fehlt, sei es das geringste in Küche oder Keller, so
weißt du was dir bevorsteht.«
I will move into it today, and if anything is missing, be it
the smallest thing in the kitchen or the cellar, you know
what lies ahead of you."

Sie trieb das Mädchen fort, und als es in das Thal kam, 4.10
so lagen da die Felsen übereinander ausgetürmt;
She drove the girl away, and when she came to the valley,
there lay the rocks piled one upon another;

4.11 mit aller seiner Kraft konnte es den kleinsten nicht einmal bewegen.
with all her strength she could not even move the smallest one.

4.12 Es setzte sich nieder und weinte,
She sat down and wept,

4.13 doch hoffte es auf den Beistand der guten Alten.
but hoped for the help of the good old woman.

4.14 Sie ließ auch nicht lange auf sich warten, kam und sprach ihm Trost ein:
She was not long in coming and consoled him:

4.15 »Lege dich nur dort in den Schatten und schlafe,
"Lie down there in the shade and sleep,

4.16 ich will dir das Schloß schon bauen. Wenn es dir Freude macht,
I will build the castle for you. If you like it,

4.17 so kannst du selbst darin wohnen.«
you can live in it yourself."

4.18 Als das Mädchen weggegangen war,
When the girl had gone away,

4.19 rührte die Alte die grauen Felsen an.
the old woman touched the gray rocks.

4.20 Alsbald regten sie sich, rückten zusammen und standen da, als hätten Riesen die Mauer gebaut;
Immediately they stirred, moved together and stood there as if giants had built the wall;

darauf erhob sich das Gebäude, und es war, als ob   4.21
unzählige Hände unsichtbar arbeiteten und Stein auf
Stein legten.
then the building rose, and it was as if countless hands were
working invisibly, laying stone upon stone.

Der Boden dröhnte,   4.22
The ground rumbled,

große Säulen stiegen von selbst in die Höhe und   4.23
stellten sich nebeneinander in Ordnung.
great pillars rose up of their own accord and lined up side
by side.

Auf dem Dache Legten sich die Ziegel zurecht,   4.24
und als es Mittag war, drehte sich schon die
große Wetterfahne wie eine goldene Jungfrau mit
fliegendem Gewand auf der Spitze des Turmes.
The tiles were being laid on the roof, and by midday the
great weathervane was spinning like a golden maiden in a
flying robe at the top of the tower.

Das Innere des Schlosses war bis zum Abend   4.25
vollendet.
The interior of the castle was finished by evening.

4.26 Wie es die Alte anfing, weiß ich nicht, aber die Wände der Zimmer waren mit Seide und Sammet bezogen, buntgestickte Stühle standen da und reichverzierte Armsessel an Tischen von Marmor; krystallene Kronleuchter hingen von der Bühne herab und spiegelten sich in dem glatten Boden; grüne Papageien saßen in goldenen Käfigen, und fremde Vögel, die lieblich sangen; überall war eine Pracht, als wenn ein König da einziehen sollte.

I do not know how the old woman began it, but the walls of the rooms were covered with silk and velvet; there were brightly embroidered chairs and richly ornamented arm-chairs at marble tables; crystalline chandeliers hung down from the stage and were reflected in the smooth floor; green parrots sat in golden cages, and strange birds sang sweetly; everywhere was a splendor as if a king were to move in.

4.27 Die Sonne wollte eben untergehen, als das Mädchen erwachte und ihm der Glanz von tausend Lichtern entgegenleuchtete.

The sun was just about to set when the girl woke up and was met by the radiance of a thousand lights.

4.28 Mit schnellen Schritten kam es heran und trat durch das geöffnete Thor in das Schloß.

She approached with quick steps and entered the castle through the open gate.

4.29 Die Treppe war mit rotem Tuch belegt und das goldene Geländer mit blühenden Bäumen besetzt.

The staircase was covered with red cloth and the golden banisters were decorated with blossoming trees.

4.30 Als es die Pracht der Zimmer erblickte,

When he saw the splendor of the rooms,

blieb es wie erstarrt stehen. 4.31
he stood frozen.

Wer weiß, wie lange es so gestanden hätte, wenn ihm nicht der Gedanke an die Stiefmutter gekommen wäre. 4.32
Who knows how long she would have stood like that if the thought of her stepmother hadn't crossed her mind.

»Ach.« sprach es zu sich selbst, 4.33
"Oh." she said to herself,

»wenn sie doch endlich zufrieden gestellt wäre und mir das Leben nicht länger zur Qual machen wollte.« 4.34
"if only she were finally satisfied and no longer wanted to make my life a misery."

Das Mädchen ging und zeigte ihr an, daß das Schloß fertig wäre. 4.35
The girl went and showed her that the castle was ready.

»Gleich will ich einziehen.« 4.36
"I will move in at once."

sagte sie und erhob sich von ihrem Sitz. 4.37
she said, and rose from her seat.

Als sie in das Schloß eintrat, mußte sie die Hand vor die Augen halten, so blendete sie der Glanz. 4.38
As she entered the castle, she had to put her hand over her eyes, for the glare blinded her.

»Siehst du.« sagte sie zu dem Mädchen, 4.39
"You see." she said to the girl,

»wie leicht dir's geworden ist, 4.40
"how easy it has become for you,

4.41 ich hätte dir etwas Schwereres aufgeben sollen.«

I should have given you something heavier."

4.42 Sie ging durch alle Zimmer und spürte in allen Ecken, ob etwas fehlte oder mangelhaft wäre, aber sie konnte nichts auffinden.

She went through all the rooms and felt in every corner to see if anything was missing or lacking, but she could find nothing.

4.43 »Jetzt wollen wir hinabsteigen.«

"Now let us go downstairs."

4.44 sprach sie und sah das Mädchen mit boshaften Blicken an,

she said, looking at the girl with a mischievous expression,

4.45 »Küche und Keller muß noch untersucht werden; und hast du etwas vergessen, so sollst du deiner Strafe nicht entgehen.«

"the kitchen and cellar must be examined, and if you have forgotten anything, you shall not escape punishment."

4.46 Aber das Feuer brannte auf dem Herd, in den Töpfen kochten, die Speisen, Kluft und Schippe waren angelehnt und an den Wänden das blanke Geschirr von Messing aufgestellt.

But the fire was burning on the hearth, the pots were boiling, the food was boiling, the ladle and shovel were ajar, and the walls were lined with bright brass dishes.

4.47 Nichts fehlte,

Nothing was missing,

4.48 selbst nicht der Kohlenkasten und die Wassereimer.

not even the coal box and the water buckets.

»Wo ist der Eingang zum Keller?« rief sie, 4.49

"Where is the entrance to the cellar?" she called,

»wenn der, nicht mit Weinfässern reichlich angefüllt 4.50
ist, so wird dir's schlimm ergehen.«

"if it isn't full of barrels of wine, you'll have a bad time."

Sie hob selbst die Fallthür auf und stieg die Treppe 4.51
hinab?;

She lifted the trap-door herself, and descended the stairs;

aber kaum hatte sie zwei Schritte gethan, so stürzte, 4.52
die schwere Fallthür, die nur angelehnt war nieder.

but she had scarcely taken two steps when the heavy trap-
door, which was only ajar, fell down.

Das Mädchen hörte einen Schrei, hob die Thür 4.53
schnell auf, um ihr zu Hilfe zu kommen, aber sie
war hinabgestürzt, und es fand sie entseelt auf dem
Boden liegen.

The girl heard a scream and quickly lifted the door to
help her, but she had fallen down and was found lying
disembodied on the floor.

Nun gehörte das prächtige Schloß dem Mädchen 5.1
ganz allein.

Now the magnificent castle belonged to the girl alone.

Es wußte sich in der ersten Zeit gar nicht in sein 5.2
Glück zu finden, schöne Kleider hingen in den
Schränken, die Truhen waren mit Gold und Silber
oder mit Perlen und Edelsteinen angefüllt, und es
hatte keinen Wunsch, den es nicht erfüllen konnte.

At first she did not know how to find her happiness,
beautiful dresses hung in the wardrobes, the chests were
filled with gold and silver or pearls and precious stones, and
she had no wish that she could not fulfill.

5.3 **Bald ging der Ruf von der Schönheit und dem Reichtum des Mädchens durch die ganze Welt.**
Soon the fame of the girl's beauty and wealth spread throughout the world.

5.4 **Alle Tage meldeten sich Freier, aber keiner gefiel ihr.**
Suitors came forward every day, but none of them pleased her.

5.5 **Endlich kam auch der Sohn eines Königs, der ihr Herz zu rühren wußte, und sie verlobte sich mit ihm.**
Finally, the son of a king came along who knew how to touch her heart, and she became engaged to him.

5.6 **In dem Schloßgarten stand eine grüne Linde;**
There was a green lime-tree in the castle garden;

5.7 **darunter saßen sie eines Tages vertraulich zusammen, da sagte er zu ihr**
one day they were sitting together under it intimately, when he said to her,

5.8 **»Ich will heimziehen und die Einwilligung meines Vaters zu unserer Vermählung holen;**
"I will go home and get my father's consent to our marriage;

5.9 **ich bitte dich, harre mein hier unter dieser Linde, in wenigen Stunden bin ich wieder zurück.«**
I beg you to wait for me here under this lime-tree, I shall be back in a few hours."

5.10 **Das Mädchen küßte ihn auf die linke Backe und sprach:**
The girl kissed him on the left cheek and said,

»Bleib, mir treu und laß dich von keiner anderen auf diese Backe küssen.

5.11

"Stay true to me and don't let anyone else kiss you on this cheek.

Ich will hier unter der Linde warten, bis du wieder zurückkommst.«

5.12

I will wait here under the lime tree until you come back."

Das Mädchen blieb unter der Linde sitzen, bis die Sonne unterging, aber er kam nicht wieder zurück.

6.1

The girl sat under the lime tree until the sun went down, but he never came back.

Sie saß drei Tage von Morgen bis Abend, und erwartete ihn, aber vergeblich.

6.2

She sat three days from morning till evening, waiting for him, but in vain.

Als er am vierten Tage noch nicht da war, so sagte sie:

6.3

When he was still not there on the fourth day, she said,

»Gewiß ist ihm ein Unglück begegnet, ich will ausgehen und ihn suchen, und nicht eher wiederkommen, als bis ich ihn gefunden habe.«

6.4

"Surely some misfortune has befallen him, I will go out and seek him, and not return until I have found him."

Sie packte drei von ihren schönsten Kleidern zusammen, eins mit glänzenden Sternen gestickt, das zweite mit silbernen Monden, das dritte mit goldenen Sonnen, band eine Hand voll Edelsteine in ihr Tuch, und machte sich auf.

6.5

She gathered together three of her most beautiful dresses, one embroidered with shining stars, the second with silver moons, the third with golden suns, tied a handful of precious stones in her shawl, and set out.

6.6 Sie fragte allerorten nach ihrem Bräutigam, aber niemand hatte ihn gesehen, niemand wußte von ihm.

She asked everywhere about her bridegroom, but no one had seen him, no one knew of him.

6.7 Weit und breit wanderte sie durch die Welt,

She wandered far and wide through the world,

6.8 aber sie fand ihn nicht. Endlich,

but she did not find him. Finally,

6.9 vermietete sie sich bei einem Bauer als Hirtin und vergrub ihre Kleider und Edelsteine unter einem Stein.

she hired herself out to a farmer as a shepherdess and buried her clothes and jewels under a stone.

7.1 Nun lebte sie als eine Hirtin, hütete ihre Herde, war traurig und voll Sehnsucht nach ihrem Geliebten.

Now she lived as a shepherdess, tended her flock, was sad and full of longing for her beloved.

7.2 Sie hatte, ein Kälbchen, das gewöhnte sie an sich, fütterte es aus der Hand, und wenn sie sprach:

She had a little calf, which she got used to, fed it from her hand, and when she spoke:

»Kalbchen, Kälbchen, knie nieder,

"Little calf, little calf, kneel down,

vergiß nicht deine Hirtin wieder,

Do not forget your shepherdess again,

wie der Königssohn die Braut vergaß,

how the king's son forgot the bride,

die unter der grünen Linde
saß.«

who sat under the green
lime tree."

so kniete das Kälbchen nieder und ward von ihr
gestreichelt.

9.1

So the little calf knelt down and was stroked by her.

Als sie ein paar Jahre einsam und kummervoll gelebt
hatte, so verbreitete sich im Lande das Gerücht, daß
die Tochter des Königs ihre Hochzeit feiern wollte.

10.1

When she had lived a few years in loneliness and sorrow, a
rumor spread through the country that the king's daughter
was going to celebrate her wedding.

Der Weg nach der Stadt ging an dem Dorfe vorbei,
wo das Mädchen wohnte, und es trug sich zu, als
sie einmal ihre Herde austrieb, daß der Bräutigam
vorüberzog.

10.2

The road to the town went past the village where the girl
lived, and it happened once, as she was driving her herd,
that the bridegroom passed by.

Er saß stolz auf seinem Pferde und sah sie nicht an;

10.3

He sat proudly on his horse, and did not look at her;

aber als sie ihn ansah, so erkannte sie ihren Liebsten.

10.4

but when she looked at him, she recognized her beloved.

Es war, als ob ihr ein scharfes Messer in das, Herz,
schnitte.

10.5

It was as if a sharp knife had cut her heart.

»Ach.« sagte sie,

10.6

"Ah." she said,

152

10.7 »ich glaubte, er wäre mir treu geblieben, aber er hat mich vergessen.«

"I thought he would have remained faithful to me, but he has forgotten me."

11.1 Am anderen Tage kam er wieder des Weges.

The next day he came along the path again.

11.2 Als er in ihrer Nähe war, sprach sie zum Kälbchen:

When he was near her, she spoke to the little calf:

»Kälbchen, Kälbchen, knie nieder,	"Little calf, little calf, kneel down,
vergiß nicht deine Hirtin wieder,	Do not forget your shepherdess again,
wie der Königssohn die Braut vergaß,	how the king's son forgot the bride,
die unter der grünen Linde saß.«	who sat under the green lime tree."

13.1 Als er die Stimme vernahm,

When he heard the voice,

13.2 blickte er herab und hielt sein Pferd an.

he looked down and stopped his horse.

13.3 Er schaute der Hirtin ins Gesicht, hielt dann die Hand vor die Augen, als wollte er sich aus etwas besinnen aber schnell ritt er weiter und war bald verschwunden.

He looked the shepherdess in the face, then held his hand in front of his eyes as if he wanted to think about something, but he quickly rode on and was soon gone.

»Ach, sagte sie, »er kennt mich nicht mehr.«

13.4

"Oh," she said, "he no longer knows me."

und ihre Trauer ward immer größer.

13.5

and her grief grew ever greater.

Bald darauf sollte an dem Hofe des Königs drei Tage lang ein großes Fest gefeiert werden,

14.1

Soon afterwards a great feast was to be held at the king's court for three days,

und das ganze Land ward dazu eingeladen.

14.2

and the whole country was invited.

»Nun will ich das letzte versuchen.«

14.3

"Now I will try the last."

dachte das Mädchen, und als der Abend kam, ging es zu dem Stein, unter dem es seine Schätze vergraben hatte.

14.4

thought the girl, and when evening came, she went to the stone under which she had buried her treasures.

Sie holte das Kleid mit den goldenen Sonnen bevor,

14.5

She fetched the dress with the golden suns,

legte es an und schmückte sich mit den Edelsteinen.

14.6

put it on and adorned herself with the precious stones.

Ihre Haare, die sie unter einem Tuche verborgen hatte, band sie auf, und sie fielen in langen Locken an ihr herab.

14.7

She untied her hair, which she had hidden under a cloth, and it fell down in long curls.

14.8 So ging sie nach der Stadt und ward in der Dunkelheit von niemand bemerkt.

So she went to the city and was not noticed by anyone in the darkness.

14.9 Als sie in den hell erleuchteten Saal trat, wichen alle voll Verwunderung zurück, aber niemand wußte, wer sie war.

When she entered the brightly-lit hall, everyone drew back in astonishment, but no one knew who she was.

14.10 Der Königssohn ging ihr entgegen, doch er erkannte sie nicht.

The king's son went to meet her, but he did not recognize her.

14.11 Er führte sie zum Tanz und war so entzückt über ihre Schönheit, daß er an die andere Braut gar nicht mehr dachte.

He led her to the dance and was so enchanted by her beauty that he did not even think about the other bride.

14.12 Als das Fest vorüber war, verschwand sie im Gedränge und eilte vor Tagesanbruch in das Dorf, wo sie ihr Hirtenkleid wieder anlegte.

When the feast was over, she disappeared into the crowd and hurried to the village before daybreak, where she put on her shepherd's dress again.

15.1 Am anderen Abend nahm sie das Kleid mit den silbernen Monden heraus und steckte einen Halbmond von Edelsteinen in ihre Haare.

The next evening she took out the dress with the silver moons and put a crescent of precious stones in her hair.

Als sie auf dem Fest sich zeigte, wendeten sich
alle Augen nach ihr, aber der Königssohn eilte ihr
entgegen, und ganz von Liebe erfüllt, tanzte er mit
ihr allein und blickte keine andere mehr an.   15.2

When she appeared at the feast, all eyes turned towards
her, but the king's son hastened to meet her, and, filled
with love, he danced with her alone and looked at no one
else.

Ehe sie wegging, mußte sie ihm versprechen, den   15.3
letzten Abend nochmals zum Fest zu kommen.

Before she went away, she had to promise him that she
would come to the feast again on the last evening.

Als sie zum drittenmal erschien, hatte sie das   16.1
Sternenkleid an, das bei jedem ihrer Schritte
funkelte, und Haarband und Gürtel waren Sterne
von Edelsteinen.

When she appeared for the third time, she was wearing the
starry dress that sparkled with every step she took, and her
hairband and belt were stars of precious stones.

Der Königssohn hatte schon, lange auf sie gewartet   16.2
und drängte sich zu ihr hin.

The king's son had been waiting for her for a long time and
pushed his way towards her.

»Sage mir nur, wer du bist.« sprach er,   16.3

"Just tell me who you are." he said,

»mir ist als wenn ich dich schon lange gekannt   16.4
hätte.«

"I feel as if I've known you for a long time."

»Weißt du nicht.« antwortete sie,   16.5

"Don't you know." she replied,

156

16.6 »was ich that, als du von mir schiedest?«
"what I did when you left me?"

16.7 Da trat sie zu ihm heran, und küßte ihn auf die linke
Backe;
Then she came up to him and kissed him on the left cheek;

16.8 in dem Augenblick fiel es wie Schuppen von seinen
Augen und er erkannte die wahre Braut.
at that moment the scales fell from his eyes and he
recognized the true bride.

16.9 »Komm.« sagte er zu ihr,
"Come." he said to her,

16.10 »hier ist meines Bleibens nicht länger.«
"this is no longer my place."

16.11 reichte ihr die Hand und führte sie hinab zu dem
Wagen.
He held out his hand to her and led her down to the
carriage.

16.12 Als wäre der Wind vorgespannt,
As if harnessed by the wind,

16.13 so eilten die Pferde zu dem Wunderschloß.
the horses hurried to the wonderful castle.

16.14 Schon von weitem glänzten die erleuchteten Fenster.
The lighted windows gleamed from afar.

Als sie bei der Linde vorbeifuhren, schwärmten unzählige Glühwürmer darin, sie schüttelte ihre Äste und sendete ihre Düste herab.

As they passed the lime-tree, innumerable glow-worms swarmed in it, it shook its branches and sent down its vapors.

Auf der Treppe blühten die Blumen, aus dem Zimmer schallte der Gesang der fremden Vögel, aber in dem Saal stand der ganze Hof versammelt und der Priester wartete, um den Bräutigam mit der wahren Braut zu vermählen.

Flowers bloomed on the staircase, the song of strange birds resounded from the room, but in the hall the whole court was assembled and the priest was waiting to marry the bridegroom to the true bride.

Der Hase und der Igel

The Hare and the Hedgehog

1.1 Disse Geschicht is lögenhaft, to vertellen, Jungens, aver wahr is se doch, denn mien Grootvader, von den ick se hew, plegg jümmer, wenn he se mie vortüerde (mit Behaglichkeit vortrug), dabi to segen:

This story is a lie to tell, boys, but it is true, because my grandfather, from whom I got it, always said when he recited it to me:

1.2 »Wahr mutt se doch sien, mien Söhn, anners kunn man se jo nich vertellen.«

"It has to be true, my son, you can't tell it any other way."

1.3 De Geschicht hett sick aber so todragen.

But the story is so true.

Et wöör an enen Sündagmorgen tor Harvesttied, 2.1
jüst as de Bookweeten bloihde, de Sünn wöör hellig
upgaen am Hewen, de Morgenwind güng warm över
de Stoppeln, de Larken süngen inn'r Lucht (Luft),
de Immen sumsten in den Bookweeten un de Lühde
güngen in ehren Sündagsstaht nah'r Kerken, un alle
Kreatur wöör vergnögt, un de Swinegel ook.

It was on a sunday morning before the harvest, just as
the bookweed was blooming, the sun was rising brightly
on the hill, the morning wind was blowing warmly over
the stubble, the larks were singing in the light (air), the
bucks were humming in the bookweed and the larks were
walking in their sunday dust near the candles, and all
creatures were happy, and the swine angels too.

De Swinegel aver stund vör siener Döhr, harr de Arm 3.1
ünnerslagen, keek dabi in den Morgenwind hinut un
quinkeleerde en lütjet Leedken vör sick hin, so good
un so slecht as nu eben am leewen Sündagmorgen en
Swinegel to singen pleggt, Indem he nu noch so half
liefe vör sick hin sung, füll em up eenmal in he künn
ook wol, mittlerwiel sien Fro de Kinner wüsch un
antröcke, en beeten in't Feld spazeeren un tosehen,
wie sien Stähkröwen stünden.

The Swinegel, however, stood in front of his door, had
his arm outstretched, was heading out into the morning
wind and sang a quiet song to himself, as good and as bad
as a Swinegel was able to sing on the last Sunday morning,
While he was still singing along, he was able to go for a
walk in the field and see how his little toads were standing.

De Stähkröwen wöören aver de nöchsten bi sienem 3.2
Huuse, un he pleggte mit siener Familie davon to
eten, darum sahg he se as de sienigen an.

However, the bull toads were the closest to his house, and
he was planning to eat there with his family, so he looked at
them as his own.

160

3.3 **Gesagt, gedahn.**

No sooner said than done.

3.4 **De Swinegel matte de Huusdöör achter sick to un slög den Weg nah'n Felde in.**

The Swinegel moved the house door behind him and slipped into the field.

3.5 **He wöör noch nich gans wiet von Huuse un wull jüst um den Glöbusch (Schlehenbusch), de dar vörm Felde liggt, nah den Stähkröwenacker hinup dreien, as em de Has bemött, de in ähnlichen Geschäften nutgahn wöör, nämlich um sienen Kohl to besehn.**

He wasn't quite far from the house yet and wanted to go around the glöbusch (blackthorn bush), which lay in front of the field, close to the Stähkröwenacker, as the hare, who was engaged in similar business, wanted to see his cabbage.

3.6 **As de Swinegel den Hasen ansichtig wöör so böhd he em en fründlichen go'n Morgen.**

When the Swinegel saw the hare, he bid him a cheerful good morning.

3.7 **De Has aver, de up siene Wies en vörnehmer Herr was, un grausahm hochfahrtig dabi, antwoorde nicks up den Swinegel sienen Gruß, sondern segte tom Swinegel, wobi he en gewaltig höhnische Miene annöhm:**

However, the hare, who was a distinguished gentleman in his field, and was very excited, did not reply to the hare's greeting, but said to the hare, making a hugely scornful face:

3.8 **»Wie kummt et denn, dat du hier all bi so frohem Morgen im Felde rumlöppst?«**

"How come you're all lolloping around in the field on such a happy morning?"

»Ick gah spazeeren.« segt de Swinegel. »Spazeeren?«   3.9
"I'm going for a walk." said the hare. "Going for a walk?"

lachte de Has,   3.10
laughed the hare,

»mi ducht, du kunnst de Veen ook wol to betern   3.11
Dingen gebrunken.«
"I think you can also bring the birds to better things."

Disse Antword verdrööt den Swinegel ungeheuer,   3.12
denn alles kunn he verdregen, aber up siene Veen
laet he nicks komen, eben weil se von Natuhr scheef
wöören.
The swine angel was incredibly put off by this answer,
because he could talk about anything, but he didn't want to
talk about his own eyes, precisely because they were from
nature.

»Du bildst di wol in.«   3.13
"You're really imagining things."

segt nu de Swinegel tom Hasen,   3.14
says the swine angel to the hare,

»as wenn du mit diene Beene mehr utrichten   3.15
kunnst?«
"as if you could do more with your legs?"

»Dat denk ick.« segt de Has. »Dat kummt up'n   3.16
Versöök an.«
"I think so." says the hare. "It depends on the verse."

meent de Swinegel,   3.17
says the swine angel,

3.18 »ick pareer, wenn wi in de Wett loopt, ick loop di
vörbi.«
"I know that when we loop in the race, I'll loop in front of
you."

3.19 »Dat is tum Lachen, du mit diene scheefen Been.«
"That's a bit of a laugh, you with your beautiful legs."

3.20 segt de Has,
says the hare,

3.21 »aver mienetwegen mach't sien, wenn du so
övergroote Lust hest.
"but I'll do it for you if you have such a big appetite.

3.22 Wat gilt de Wett?«
What's the bet?"

3.23 »En goldne Lujedor un'n Buddel Branwien.« segt de
Swinegel.
"A golden lujedor and a bottle of branwien." says the
Swinegel.

3.24 »Angenahmen.« spröök de Has, »sla in,
"Accept." says the hare, "slap it in,

3.25 un denn kann't gliek los gahn.«
and then you're good to go."

3.26 »Nä, so groote Ihl hett et nich.« meen de Swinegel,
"Well, it's not that big." says the swine angel,

3.27 »ick bün noch gans nüchdern;
"I'm still quite new;

3.28 eerst will ick to Huus gahn un en beeten fröhstücken,
first I want to go home and have a nice breakfast,

inner halwen Stünd bün ick wedder hier upp'n Platz.«

3.29

and within half an hour I'll be back here in my seat."

Damit güng de Swinegel, denn de Has wöör et tofreeden.

4.1

The Swinegel went with it, because the hare would love it.

Ünnerwegs dachte de Swinegel bi sick:

4.2

On the way, the swine angel thought to himself:

»De Has verlett sick up siene langen Been,

4.3

"The hare is getting up on his long legs,

aver ick will em wol kriegen.

4.4

but I want to get him.

He is zwar ehn vörnehm Herr, aver doch man'n dummen Keerl, un betahlen sall he doch.«

4.5

He may be a gentleman, but he's a silly little fellow and he has to pay."

As nu de Swinegel to Huuse ankööm, spröök he to sien Fro:

4.6

When the swine angel arrived at his house, he said to his wife:

»Fro, treck die gau (schnell) an, du must mit mi nah'n Felde hinuut.«

4.7

"Fro, get them on quickly, you have to go with me to the field."

»Wat givt et denn?« segt sien Fro.

4.8

"What's there then?" says his friend.

4.9 »Ick hew mit'n Hasen wett't üm'n golden Lujedor un'n Buddel Branwien, ick will mit em inn Wett loopen, un da salst du mit dabi sien.«

"I've bet with a hare for a golden lujedor and a bottle of branwien, I want to run with him in a race, and you have to be there with me."

4.10 »O mien Gott, Mann.«

"Oh my God, man."

4.11 füng nu den Swinegel sien Fro an to schreen,

the Swinegel now began to shout to his wife,

4.12 »büst do nich klook, hest du denn ganz den Verstand verlaaren?

"aren't you clever, have you lost your mind completely?

4.13 Wie kannst du mit den Hasen in de Wett loopen wollen?«

How can you want to run with the hares in the race?"

4.14 »Holt dat Muul, Wief.« segt de Swinegel, »dat is mien Saak.

"Get your mouth, Wief." says the Swinegel, "that's my job.

4.15 Resonehr nich in Männergeschäfte. Marsch,

Don't go into men's business. Come on,

4.16 treck di an un denn kumm mit.«

get dressed and then come with me."

4.17 Wat sull den Swinegel sien Fro maken? Se mußt wol folgen,

What should the Swinegel's wife do? She must follow,

4.18 se mugg nu wollen oder nich.

she may want to or not.

As se nu miteenander ünnerwegs wöören,   5.1
As they were walking along together,

spröök de Swinegel to sien Fro: 5.2
the Swinegel spoke to his wife:

»Nu paß up, wat ick seggen will. Sühst du,   5.3
"Now pay attention to what I want to say. You see,

up den langen Acker dar wüll wi unsen Wettloop   5.4
maken.
we want to make our bet on the long field there.

De Has löppt nemlich in der eenen Föhr (Furche) un   5.5
ick inner andern,
The hare is loafing in one furrow and I'm in the other,

un von baben (oben) fang wie an to loopen.   5.6
and we'll start loafing from the top.

Nu hast du wieder nicks to dohn, as du stellst di hier   5.7
unnen in de Föhr, un wenn de Haas up de andere Siet
ankummt, so röpst du em entgegen:
Now you have nothing to do again, as you stand here in the
furrow, and when the hare arrives on the other side, you
shout to him:

»Ick bin all (schon) hier.«   5.8
"I'm all (already) here."

Damit wöören se bi den Acker anlangt, de Swinegel   6.1
wiesde siener Fro ehren Platz an, un gung nu den
Acker hinup.
They arrived at the field, the Swinegel showed his friend his
place and walked up the field.

6.2 As he baben ankööm, wöör de Has all da. »Kann et losgahn?«

When he arrived, the hares were all there. "Can we start?"

6.3 segt de Has. »Jawol.« segt de Swinegel.

said the hare. "Yes, yes." said the swine angel.

6.4 »Denn man to!« Un damit stellde jeder sick in siene Föhr.

"Then you go!" And with that, everyone stood in their place.

6.5 De Has tellde (zählte): »Hahl een, hahl twee, hahl dree.«

The hare told (counted): "Hahl een, hahl twee, hahl dree."

6.6 un los güng he wie en Stormwind den Acker hindahl (hinab).

And off he went like a storm wind down the field.

6.7 De Swinegel aver lööp ungefähr man dree Schritt,

But the Swinegel took about three steps,

6.8 dann duhkde he sick dahl (herab) in de Führ un bleev ruhig sitten.

then he went down the path and sat quietly.

7.1 As nu de Has in vullen Loopen ünnen am Acker ankööm,

When the hare arrived at the field in all its loops,

7.2 rööp em den Swinegel sien Fro entgegen: »Ick bün all hier.«

the swine angel called out to him: "I'm all here."

7.3 De Has stutzd un verwunderde sick nich wenig:

The hare was taken aback and not a little surprised:

he meende nich anders als et wöör de Swinegel 7.4
sülvst, de em dat torööp, denn bekanntlich süht
den Swinegel sien Fro jüst so uut wie ehr Mann.
he didn't think it was the swine angel himself who had
called out to him, because, as we all know, the swine
angel's wife looks just like her husband.

De Has aver meende: 7.5
But the man said:

»Datt geiht nich to mit rechten Dingen.« He rööp: 7.6
"That's not right." He shouted:

»Nochmal geloopen, wedder üm!« 7.7
"Looped again, around again!"

Un fort güng he wedder wie en Stormwind, 7.8
And off he went again like a gale-force wind,

dat em de Ohren am Koppe flögen. 7.9
his ears flying off his head.

Den Swinegel sien Fro aver blev ruhig up ehren 7.10
Platze.
But the Swinegel's wife remained calmly in her place.

As nu de Has baben ankööm, roop em de Swinegel 7.11
entgegen:
When the hare arrived, the swine angel called out to him:

»Ick bün all hier.« 7.12
"I'm all here."

De Has aver, ganz uuter sick vör Ihwer (Ärger), 7.13
schreede:
But the hare, full of himself (anger), shouted:

7.14 »Nochmal geloopen, wedder üm!«
"Open again, around again!"

7.15 »Mi nich to schlimm.« antwoorde de Swinegel,
"Not too bad." replied the Swinegel,

7.16 »mienetwegen so oft as du Lust hest.«
"as often as you feel like it."

7.17 So löp de Has noch dreeunsöbentigmal,
And so the rabbit lolled three dozen more times,

7.18 un de Swinegel höhl (hielt) et ümmer mit em uut.
and the swine angel kept up with him.

7.19 Jedesmal, wenn de Has ünnen oder baben ankööm, segten de Swinegel oder sien Fro:
Every time the hare arrived in the morning or evening, the swine angel or his wife would say:

7.20 »Ick bün all hier.«
"I'm all here."

8.1 Tum veerunsöbentigstenmal aver küm de Has nich mehr to ende.
But at the most inopportune moment, the hare can no longer finish.

8.2 Midden am Acker stört he tor Eerde, datt Blohd flög em utn Halse un he bleev doot upn Platze.
In the middle of the field, he stumbled over the ground, his blood flew out of his throat and he stayed put.

De Swinegel aver nöhm siene gewunnene Lujedor un den Buddel Branwien, rööp siene Fra uut der Föhr aff, un beide güngen vergnögt mit eenanner nah Huus; 8.3

But the Swinegel took his won Lujedor and the Buddel Branwien, called his wife from the Föhr, and both went happily to the house with one another;

un wenn se nich storben sünd, lewt se noch. 8.4

and if they didn't die, they were still alive.

So begev et sick, dat up der Buxtehuder Heid de Swinegel den Hasen dodt lopen hett, un sied jener Tied hatt et sick keen Has wedder infallen laten mit'n Buxtehuder Swinegel in de Wett to lopen. 9.1

So it happened that on the Buxtehude heath, the swine bird killed the hare, and at that time no hare fell in love with the Buxtehude swine bird.

De Lehre aver uut disser Geschicht is erstens, datt keener, un wenn he sick ook noch so vörnehm dücht, sick sall bikommen laten, övern geringen Mann sick lustig to maken, un wöört ook man'n Swinegel. 10.1

But the lesson of this story is, firstly, that no one, no matter how self-important he may think he is, should be allowed to make fun of a small man, and he is also called a swine angel.

Un tweetens, datt et gerahden is, wenn eener freet, datt he sick 'ne Fro uut sienem Stande nimmt, un de jüst so uutsüht as he sülwst. 10.2

And tweet that it is right when someone frees himself to take a wife from his station, and that she looks just like he does.

10.3 **Wer also en Swinegel is, de mutt tosehn, datt siene Fro ook en Swinegel is, un so wieder.**

So whoever is a swine angel must see that his wife is also a swine angel, and so on.

Spindel, Weberschiffchen and Nadel

Spindle, Shuttle and Needle

1.1 **Es war einmal ein Mädchen, dem starb Vater und Mutter, als es noch ein kleines Kind war.**

Once upon a time there was a girl whose father and mother died when she was still a small child.

1.2 **Am Ende des Dorfes wohnte in einem Häuschen ganz allein seine Pate, die sich von Spinnen, Weben und Nähen ernährte.**

Her godmother lived alone in a little house at the end of the village, supporting herself by spinning, weaving and sewing.

1.3 **Die Alte nahm das verlassene Kind zu sich,**

The old woman took the abandoned child in,

1.4 **hielt es zur Arbeit an und erzog es in aller Frömmigkeit.**

put her to work and brought her up in all piety.

Als das Mädchen fünfzehn Jahre alt war, erkrankte
sie, rief das Kind an ihr Bett und sagte:

1.5

When the girl was fifteen years old, she fell ill, called the
child to her bed and said:

»Liebe Tochter, ich fühle, daß mein Ende herannaht,
ich hinterlasse dir das Häuschen, darin bist du
vor Wind und Wetter geschützt, dazu Spindel,
Weberschiffchen und Nadel, damit kannst du dir
dein Brot verdienen.«

1.6

"Dear daughter, I feel that my end is approaching, I leave
you the little house, in which you are protected from wind
and weather, plus spindle, shuttle and needle, with which
you can earn your bread."

Sie legte noch die Hände auf seinen Kopf,

1.7

She laid her hands on his head,

segnete es und sprach:

1.8

blessed it and said:

»Behalt nur Gott in dem Herzen, so wird dir's wohl
gehen.«

1.9

"Just keep God in your heart and you will be well."

Darauf schloß sie die Augen, und als sie zur Erde
bestattet wurde, ging das Mädchen bitterlich
weinend hinter dem Sarge und erwies ihr die letzte
Ehre.

1.10

Then she closed her eyes, and when she was buried, the girl
went behind the coffin, weeping bitterly, and paid her last
respects.

2.1 Das Mädchen lebte nun in dem kleinen Haus ganz allein, war fleißig, spann, webte und nähte, und auf allem, was es that, ruhte der Segen der guten Alten.

The girl now lived all alone in the little house, was industrious, spun, wove and sewed, and on everything she did rested the blessing of the good old woman.

2.2 Es war, als ob sich der Flachs in der Kammer von selbst mehrte, und wenn sie ein Stück Tuch oder einen Teppich gewebt, oder ein Hemd genäht hatte, so fand sich gleich ein Käufer, der es reichlich bezahlte, sodaß sie keine Not empfand und anderen noch etwas mitteilen konnte.

It was as if the flax in the room multiplied by itself, and when she had woven a piece of cloth or a carpet, or sewn a shirt, a buyer was immediately found who paid handsomely for it, so that she felt no need and could still give something to others.

3.1 Um diese Zeit zog der Sohn des Königs im Lande umher und wollte sich eine Braut suchen.

Around this time, the king's son was traveling around the country and wanted to find himself a bride.

3.2 Eine arme sollte er nicht wählen und eine reiche wollte er nicht.

He should not choose a poor one and he did not want a rich one.

3.3 Da sprach er:

So he said,

3.4 »Die soll meine Frau werden, die zugleich die Ärmste und die Reichste ist.«

"She shall be my wife who is both the poorest and the richest."

Als er in das Dorf kam, wo das Mädchen lebte, fragte   3.5
er, wie er überall that, wer in dem Ort die Reichste
und die Ärmste wäre.

When he came to the village where the girl lived, he asked,
as he did everywhere, who was the richest and poorest in
the village.

Sie nannten ihm die Reichste zuerst;   3.6

They told him the richest first;

die Ärmste, sagten sie, wäre das Mädchen, das in dem   3.7
kleinen Haus ganz am Ende wohnte.

the poorest, they said, was the girl who lived in the little
house at the end.

Die Reiche saß vor der Hausthür in vollem Putz, und   3.8
als der Königssohn sich näherte, stand sie auf, ging
ihm entgegen und neigte sich vor ihm.

The richest was sitting at the door of the house in all her
finery, and when the king's son approached, she got up,
went to meet him and bowed to him.

Er sah sie an, sprach kein Wort und ritt weiter.   3.9

He looked at her, said not a word and rode on.

Als er zu dem Haus der Armen kam, stand das   3.10
Mädchen nicht an der Thür, sondern saß in seinem
Stübchen.

When he came to the poor woman's house, the girl was not
standing at the door, but was sitting in her little room.

Er hielt das Pferd an und sah durch das Fenster,   3.11
durch das die helle Sonne schien, das Mädchen an
dem Spinnrad sitzen und emsig spinnen.

He stopped the horse and through the window, through
which the bright sun was shining, he saw the girl sitting at
the spinning wheel, busily spinning.

3.12 Es blickte auf, und als es bemerkte, daß der Königssohn hereinschaute, ward es über und über rot, schlug die Augen nieder und spann weiter;

She looked up, and when she noticed that the King's son was looking in, she blushed all over, cast down her eyes, and went on spinning;

3.13 ob der Faden diesmal ganz gleich ward, weiß ich nicht, aber es spann so lange, bis der Königssohn wieder weggeritten war.

whether the thread was quite even this time I do not know, but she spun till the King's son had ridden away again.

3.14 Dann trat es ans Fenster, öffnete es und sagte,

Then he went to the window, opened it, and said,

3.15 »Es ist so heiß in der Stube.«

"It is so hot in the parlor."

3.16 aber es blickte ihm nach, so lange es noch die weißen Federn an seinem Hut erkennen konnte.

but he looked after him as long as he could still see the white feathers on his hat.

4.1 Das Mädchen setzte sich wieder in seine Stube zur Arbeit und spann weiter.

The girl sat down to work again in her room and continued to spin.

4.2 Da kam ihm ein Spruch in den Sinn, den die Alte manchmal gesagt hatte, wenn es bei der Arbeit saß, und es sang so vor sich hin:

Then a saying came into her mind that the old woman had sometimes said when she was sitting at work, and she sang it to herself:

»Spindel, Spindel, geh du aus,

"Spindle, spindle, you go out,

bring den Freier in mein Haus.«

bring the suitor into my house."

Was geschah? 6.1
What happened?

Die Spindel sprang ihm augenblicklich aus der Hand zur Thür hinaus; 6.2
The spindle immediately sprang from his hand out of the door;

und als es vor Verwunderung aufstand und ihr nachblickte, so sah es, daß sie lustig in das Feld hineintanzte und einen glänzenden goldenen Faden hinter sich herzog. 6.3
and when he stood up in astonishment and looked after it, he saw that it was dancing merrily into the field, dragging a shining golden thread behind it.

Nicht lange, so war sie ihm aus den Augen entschwunden. 6.4
It was not long before she had disappeared from his sight.

Das Mädchen, da es keine Spindel mehr hatte, nahm das Weberschiffchen in die Hand, setzte sich an den Webstuhl und fing an zu weben. 6.5
The girl, having no more spindle, took the shuttle in her hand, sat down at the loom and began to weave.

Die Spindel aber tanzte immer weiter, und eben als der Faden zu Ende war, hatte sie den Königssohn erreicht. 7.1
But the spindle danced on and on, and just as the thread came to an end, it reached the king's son.

7.2 »Was sehe ich?« rief er,
"What do I see?" he cried,

7.3 »die Spindel will mir wohl den Weg zeigen?«
"the spindle will show me the way?"

7.4 drehte sein Pferd um und ritt an dem goldenen Faden zurück.
He turned his horse around and rode back along the golden thread.

7.5 Das Mädchen aber saß an seiner Arbeit und sang:
But the girl sat at her work and sang:

»Schiffchen, Schiffchen, webe fein,	"Shuttle, shuttle, weave finely,
führ den Freier mir herein.«	Show me the suitor in."

9.1 Alsbald sprang ihr das Schiffchen aus der Hand und sprang zur Thür hinaus.
Immediately the little boat jumped out of her hand and sprang out of the door.

9.2 Vor der Thürschwelle aber fing es an einen Teppich zu weben, schöner als man je einen gesehen hat.
But before the threshold she began to weave a carpet more beautiful than any one had ever seen.

Auf beiden Seiten blühten Rosen und Lilien und in 9.3
der Mitte auf goldenem Grund stiegen grüne Ranken
herauf, darin sprangen Hasen und Kaninchen,
Hirsche und Rehe streckten die Köpfe dazwischen,
oben in den Zweigen saßen bunte Vögel;

On both sides bloomed roses and lilies, and in the middle,
on a golden ground, rose green vines, in which hares
and rabbits leaped, stags and deer stretched their heads
between them, and colorful birds sat in the branches above;

es fehlte nichts als daß sie gesungen hätten. 9.4

nothing was wanting but that they should have sung.

Das Schiffchen sprang hin und her, 9.5

The little boat jumped to and fro,

und es war als wüchse alles von selber. 9.6

and it was as if everything grew by itself.

Weil das Schiffchen fortgelaufen war, hatte sich das 10.1
Mädchen zum Nähen hingesetzt, es hielt die Nadel in
der Hand und sang:

Because the little boat had run away, the girl had sat down
to sew, holding the needle in her hand and singing:

»Nadel, Nadel, spitz und
fein,

"Needle, needle, sharp
and fine,

mach das Haus dem Freier
rein.«

make the house clean for
the suitor."

Da sprang ihr die Nadel aus den Fingern und flog in 12.1
der Stube hin und her, so schnell wie der Blitz.

Then the needle jumped out of her fingers and flew back
and forth in the room as fast as lightning.

12.2 Es war nicht anders als wenn unsichtbare Geister
arbeiteten, alsbald überzogen sich Tisch und Bänke
mit grünem Tuch, die Stühle mit Sammet, und an
den Fenstern hingen seidene Vorhänge herab.

It was as if invisible spirits were at work; the table and
benches were soon covered with green cloth, the chairs
with velvet, and silken curtains hung down from the
windows.

12.3 Kaum hatte die Nadel den letzten Stich gethan,
so sah das Mädchen schon durch das Fenster die
weißen Federn von dem Hut des Königssohns, den die
Spindel an dem goldenen Faden herbeigeholt hatte.

The needle had scarcely made its last stitch when the girl
saw through the window the white feathers of the king's
son's hat, which the spindle had brought in by the golden
thread.

12.4 Er stieg ab, schritt über den Teppich in das Haus
herein, und als er in die Stube trat, stand das
Mädchen da in seinem ärmlichen Kleid, aber es
glühte darin wie eine Rose im Busch.

He dismounted, walked across the carpet into the house,
and when he entered the parlor, the girl stood there in her
poor dress, but glowing like a rose in a bush.

12.5 »Du bist die Ärmste und auch die Reichste.«

"You are the poorest and also the richest."

12.6 sprach er zu ihr, »komm mit mir,

he said to her, "come with me,

12.7 du sollst meine Braut sein.« Sie schwieg,

you shall be my bride." She was silent,

12.8 aber sie reichte ihm die Hand.

but she held out her hand to him.

Da gab er ihr einen Kuß, führte sie hinaus, hob sie auf   12.9
sein Pferd und brachte sie in das königliche Schloß,
wo die Hochzeit mit großer Freude gefeiert ward.

Then he kissed her, led her out, mounted her on his horse,
and took her to the royal palace, where the wedding was
celebrated with great joy.

Spindel,   12.10

The spindle,

Weberschiffchen und Nadel wurden in der   12.11
Schatzkammer verwahrt und in großen Ehren
gehalten.

shuttle and needle were kept in the treasury and held in
great honor.

Der Bauer und der Teufel

The Farmer and the Devil

1.1 **Es war einmal ein kluges und verschmitztes Bäuerlein, von dessen Streichen viel zu erzählen wäre:**

Once upon a time there was a clever and mischievous little farmer whose pranks are worth telling:

1.2 **die schönste Geschichte ist aber doch, wie er den Teufel einmal daran gekriegt und zum Narren gehabt hat.**

the best story, however, is how he once got the devil and made a fool of him.

2.1 **Das Bäuerlein hatte eines Tages seinen Acker bestellt und rüstete sich zur Heimfahrt, als die Dämmerung schon eingetreten war.**

One day the little farmer had tilled his field and was preparing to go home when dusk had already fallen.

Da erblickte er mitten auf seinem Acker 2.2
einen Haufen feuriger Kohlen, und als er voll
Verwunderung hinzuging, so saß oben auf der Glut
ein kleiner schwarzer Teufel.

Then he saw a pile of fiery coals in the middle of his field,
and when he walked over to them in amazement, he saw a
little black devil sitting on top of the embers.

»Du sitzest wohl auf einem Schatz?« 2.3

"You're sitting on a treasure, aren't you?"

sprach das Bäuerlein. »Jawohl.« antwortete der 2.4
Teufel,

said the little farmer. "Yes." replied the devil,

»auf einem Schatz, der mehr Gold und Silber enthält 2.5
als du dein Lebtag gesehen hast.«

"on a treasure that contains more gold and silver than you
have ever seen in your life."

»Der Schatz liegt auf meinem Feld und gehört mir.« 2.6

"The treasure is in my field and belongs to me."

sprach das Bäuerlein. »Er ist dein.« antwortete der 2.7
Teufel,

said the little farmer. "It is yours." replied the devil,

»wenn du mir zwei Jahre lang die Hälfte von dem 2.8
giebst, was dein Acker hervorbringt:

"if you give me half of what your field produces for two
years:

Geld habe ich genug, 2.9

I have enough money,

184

2.10 aber ich trage Verlangen nach den Früchten der
Erde.«

but I long for the fruits of the earth."

2.11 Das Bäuerlein ging auf den Handel ein.

The little farmer agreed to the deal.

2.12 »Damit aber kein Streit bei der Teilung entsteht.«
sprach es,

"But so that there is no dispute about the division." he said,

2.13 »so soll dir gehören, was über der Erde ist, und mir,
was unter der Erde ist.«

"what is above the ground shall be yours, and what is below
the ground shall be mine."

2.14 Dem Teufel gefiel das wohl,

The devil liked that,

2.15 aber das listige Bäuerlein hatte Rüben gesät.

but the cunning little farmer had sown turnips.

2.16 Als nun die Zeit der Ernte kam, so erschien der Teufel
und wollte seine Frucht holen, er fand aber nichts als
die gelben welken Blätter, und das Bäuerlein, ganz
vergnügt, grub seine Rüben aus.

When harvest time came, the devil appeared and wanted to
get his fruit, but he found nothing but the yellow withered
leaves, and the little farmer, quite happy, dug up his
turnips.

2.17 »Einmal hast du den Vorteil gehabt.« sprach der
Teufel,

"You had the advantage once." said the devil,

2.18 »aber für das nächste Mal soll das nicht gelten.

"but that won't be the case next time.

Dein ist, was über der Erde wächst, und mein, was darunter ist.«   2.19
What grows above the ground is yours, and what grows below it is mine."

»Mir auch recht.« antwortete das Bäuerlein.   2.20
"That's fine by me." replied the little farmer.

Als aber die Zeit zur Aussaat kam, säte das Bäuerlein nicht wieder Rüben, sondern Weizen.   2.21
But when the time came to sow, the farmer did not sow turnips again, but wheat.

Die Frucht ward reif,   2.22
The crop was ripe,

das Bäuerlein ging auf den Acker und schnitt die vollen Halme bis zur Erde ab.   2.23
the farmer went out into the field and cut the full stalks down to the ground.

Als der Teufel kam,   2.24
When the devil came,

fand er nichts als die Stoppeln und fuhr wütend in eine Felsenschlucht hinab.   2.25
he found nothing but the stubble and went down angrily into a rocky ravine.

»So muß man die Füchse prellen.«   2.26
"That's the way to bruise the foxes."

sprach das Bäuerlein, ging hin und holte sich den Schatz.   2.27
said the little farmer, and went and fetched the treasure.

Die Brosamen auf dem Tisch

The Crumbs on the Table

1.1 Der Güggel het einisch zue sine Hüendlene gseit:
The goose once said to his chickens:

1.2 »Chömmet weidli i dStuben ufe goh Brotbrösmele zämmebicke ufem Tisch,
"Come back to the parlor to make some bread crumbs on the table,

1.3 euse Frau isch ußgange goh ne Visite mache.«
our wife has gone out to make a visit."

1.4 Do säge do dHüendli:
Then the chicken says:

1.5 »Nei, nei, mer chömme nit, weist dFrau balget amme mit is.«
"No, no, we're not coming, the wife is coming with us."

1.6 Do seit der Güggel:
Then the goose says:

»Se weiß jo nüt dervo, chömmet er numme, se git is
doch au nie nit guets.«

"She doesn't know anything about it, he's just coming,
she's never good."

Do säge dHüendli wider:

Then the chicken says again:

»Nei, nei, sisch uß und verby, mer gönd nit ufe.«

"No, no, it's out and about, we're not going up."

Aber der Güggel het ene kei ruei glo, bis se endlig
gange sind und ufe Tisch, und do Brotbrösmeli
zämme gläse hend in aller Strenge.

But the goose didn't give them any rest until they had
finally gone to the table and were eating breadcrumbs
together.

Do chunt justement dFrau derzue und nimmt
gschwind e Stäcke und steubt se abe und regiert gar
grüseli mit ene.

Then the woman comes over and quickly picks up a stick
and pushes it down and has a nice chat with her.

Und wo se do vor em hus unde gsi sind,

And as they were standing in front of the house,

so säge do dHüendli zum Güggel:

the chicken said to the goose:

»Gse gse gse gse gse gse gsehst aber?«

"But do you see?"

Do het der Güggel glachet und numme gseit:

Then the goose smiled and said:

1.16 »Ha ha han is nit gwüßt?« Do händ se chönne goh.

"Ha ha, I didn't know?" Then they could go.

Das Meerhäschen

The Sea Bunny

1.1 Es war einmal eine Königstochter, die hatte in ihrem Schloß hoch unter der Zinne einen Saal mit zwölf Fenstern, die gingen nach allen Himmelsgegenden, und wenn sie hinaufstieg und umherschaute, so konnte sie ihr ganzes Reich übersehen.

Once upon a time, there was a princess who had a hall in her castle high below the battlements with twelve windows that looked out to all parts of the sky, and when she climbed up and looked around, she could see her entire kingdom.

1.2 Aus dem ersten sah sie schon schärfer als andere Menschen, in dem zweiten noch besser, in dem dritten noch deutlicher und so immer weiter bis in dem zwölften, wo sie alles sah, was über und unter der Erde war und ihr nichts verborgen bleiben konnte.

From the first she saw more clearly than other people, in the second even better, in the third even more clearly and so on until she reached the twelfth, where she saw everything above and below the earth and nothing could remain hidden from her.

Weil sie aber stolz war, sich niemand unterwerfen und die Herrschaft allein behalten wollte, so ließ sie bekannt machen, es sollte niemand ihr Gemahl werden, der sich nicht so vor ihr verstecken könnte, daß es ihr unmöglich wäre ihn zu finden. **1.3**

But because she was proud, did not want to submit to anyone and wanted to keep her rule alone, she made it known that no one was to become her husband who could not hide himself from her in such a way that it would be impossible for her to find him.

Wer es aber versuche und sie entdecke ihn, so werde ihm das Haupt abgeschlagen und auf einen Pfahl gesteckt. **1.4**

But whoever tried and she discovered him would have his head cut off and be put on a stake.

Es standen schon siebenundneunzig Pfähle mit toten Häuptern vor dem Schloß, **1.5**

There were already ninety-seven stakes with dead heads in front of the castle,

und in langer Zeit meldete sich niemand. **1.6**

and in a long time no one came forward.

Die Königstochter war vergnügt und dachte: **1.7**

The king's daughter was delighted and thought:

»Ich werde nun für mein Lebtag frei bleiben.« **1.8**

"I shall now remain free for the rest of my life."

Da erschienen drei Brüder vor ihr und kündigten ihr an, daß sie ihr Glück versuchen wollten. **1.9**

Then three brothers appeared before her and announced that they wanted to try their luck.

1.10 Der älteste glaubte sicher zu sein, wenn er in ein Kalkloch krieche, aber sie erblickte ihn schon aus dem ersten Fenster, ließ ihn herausziehen und ihm das Haupt abschlagen.

The eldest thought he would be safe if he crawled into a lime-hole, but she caught sight of him from the first window, had him pulled out and had his head cut off.

1.11 Der zweite kroch in den Keller des Schlosses, aber auch diesen erblickte sie aus dem ersten Fenster, und es war um ihn geschehen, sein Haupt kam auf den neunundneunzigsten Pfahl.

The second crawled into the cellar of the castle, but she also caught sight of him from the first window, and it was over for him, his head went on the ninety-ninth pole.

1.12 Da trat der jüngste vor sie hin und bat, sie möchte ihm einen Tag Bedenkzeit geben, auch so gnädig sein, es ihm zweimal zu schenken, wenn sie ihn entdecke;

Then the youngest came before her and begged her to give him a day's consideration, and to be gracious enough to give it to him twice if she discovered him;

1.13 mißlinge es ihm zum drittenmal,

if he failed the third time,

1.14 so wolle er sich nichts mehr aus seinem Leben machen.

he would make nothing more of his life.

1.15 Weil er so schön war und so herzlich bat, so sagte sie:

Because he was so beautiful and asked so sincerely, she said,

1.16 »Ja, ich will dir das bewilligen, aber es wird dir nicht glücken.«

"Yes, I will grant you that, but you will not succeed."

Den folgenden Tag sann er lange nach, wie er sich
versteicken wollte, aber es war vergeblich. 2.1

The next day he pondered for a long time how he was going
to hide, but it was in vain.

Da ergriff er seine Büchse und ging hinaus auf die
Jagd: 2.2

Then he seized his rifle and went out hunting:

Er sah einen Raben und nahm ihn aufs Korn; 2.3

he saw a raven and took aim at it;

eben wollte er losdrücken, da rief der Rabe, 2.4

just as he was about to shoot, the raven called out,

»Schieß nicht, ich will dir's vergelten!« 2.5

"Don't shoot, I will repay you!"

Er setzte ab, ging weiter und kam an einen See, wo
er einen großen Fisch überraschte, der aus der Tiefe
herauf an die Oberfläche des Wassers gekommen
war. 2.6

He set off, walked on and came to a lake, where he
surprised a large fish that had come up from the depths
to the surface of the water.

Als er angelegt hatte, rief der Fisch: »Schieß nicht, 2.7

When he had landed, the fish called out: "Don't shoot,

ich will dir's vergelten!« 2.8

I will repay you!"

Er ließ ihn untertauchen, ging weiter und begegnete
einem Fuchs, der hinkte. 2.9

He let him go under, went on and came across a fox that
was limping.

2.10 Er schoß und verfehlte ihn, da rief der Fuchs:
He shot and missed, so the fox called out:

2.11 »Komm lieber her und zieh mir den Dorn aus dem
Fuß.«
"You'd better come here and pull the thorn out of my foot."

2.12 Er that es zwar,
He did so,

2.13 wollte aber dann den Fuchs töten und ihm den Balg
abziehen.
but then wanted to kill the fox and pull off its bellows.

2.14 Der Fuchs sprach: »Laß ab, ich will dir's vergelten!«
The fox said, "Let go, I will repay you!"

2.15 Der Jüngling ließ ihn laufen, und da es Abend war,
kehrte er heim.
The youth let him go, and when evening came, he returned
home.

3.1 Am anderen Tage sollte er sich verkriechen, aber wie
er sich auch den Kopf darüber zerbrach, er wußte
nicht wohin.
The next day he was told to crawl away, but no matter how
he racked his brains, he did not know where to go.

3.2 Er ging in den Wald zu dem Raben und sprach:
He went into the forest to the raven and said,

3.3 »Ich habe dich leben lassen, jetzt sage mir, wohin ich
mich verkriechen soll, damit mich die Königstochter
nicht sieht.«
"I have let you live, now tell me where I should hide so that
the king's daughter does not see me."

Der Rabe senkte den Kopf und bedachte sich lange. 3.4
The raven bowed his head and pondered for a long time.

Endlich schnarrte er: »Ich hab's heraus!« 3.5
Finally he croaked: "I've figured it out!"

Er holte ein Ei aus seinem Nest, 3.6
He took an egg out of his nest,

zerlegte es in zwei Teile und schloß den Jüngling 3.7
hinein;
cut it in two and put the youngster inside;

dann machte er es wieder ganz und setzte sich darauf. 3.8
then he made it whole again and sat on it.

Als die Königstochter an das erste Fenster trat, 3.9
konnte sie ihn nicht entdecken, auch nicht in den
folgenden, und es fing an ihr bange zu werden, doch
im elften erblickte sie ihn.
When the King's daughter came to the first window, she
could not see him, nor could she see him in the next, and
she began to be afraid, but in the eleventh she caught sight
of him.

Sie ließ den Raben schießen, das Ei holen 3.10
und zerbrechen, und der Jüngling mußte
herauskommen.
She had the raven shot, the egg fetched and broken, and the
youth had to come out.

Sie sprach: 3.11
She said,

3.12 »Einmal ist es dir geschenkt, wenn du es nicht besser machst, so bist du verloren.«

"Once it is given to you, if you do not do better, you are lost."

4.1 Am folgenden Tage ging er an den See,

The next day he went to the lake,

4.2 rief den Fisch herbei und sprach:

called the fish and said:

4.3 »Ich habe dich leben lassen, nun sage, wohin soll ich mich verbergen, damit mich die Königstochter nicht sieht.«

"I have let you live, now tell me where I should hide so that the king's daughter does not see me."

4.4 Der Fisch besann sich, endlich rief er:

The fish came to his senses and finally called out:

4.5 »Ich hab's heraus! Ich will dich in meinen Bauch verschließen.«

"I've found out! I want to shut you up in my belly."

4.6 Er verschluckte ihn und fuhr hinab auf den Grund des Sees.

He swallowed it and went down to the bottom of the lake.

4.7 Die Königstochter blickte durch ihre Fenster, auch im elften sah sie ihn nicht und war bestürzt, doch endlich im zwölften entdeckte sie ihn.

The king's daughter looked through her windows, even in the eleventh she did not see him and was dismayed, but finally in the twelfth she discovered him.

4.8 Sie ließ den Fisch fangen und töten,

She had the fish caught and killed,

und der Jüngling kam zum Vorschein. 4.9
and the young man emerged.

Es kann sich jeder denken, wie ihm zu Mute war. Sie sprach, 4.10
Everyone can imagine how he felt. She said,

»Zweimal ist dir's geschenkt, 4.11
"Twice it is given you,

aber dein Haupt wird wohl auf den hundertsten Pfahl kommen.« 4.12
but your head will probably go on the hundredth stake."

An dem letzten Tage ging er mit schwerem Herzen aufs Feld und begegnete dem Fuchs. 5.1
On the last day, he went out into the field with a heavy heart and met the fox.

»Du weißt alle Schlupfwinkel zu finden.« sprach er, 5.2
"You know how to find every hiding place." he said,

»ich habe dich leben lassen, jetzt rate mir, wohin ich mich verstecken soll, damit mich die Königstochter nicht findet.« 5.3
"I have let you live, now tell me where I should hide so that the king's daughter does not find me."

»Ein schweres Stück.« antwortete der Fuchs, 5.4
"That's a hard one." answered the fox,

und machte ein bedenkliches Gesicht. Endlich rief er, 5.5
making a troubled face. At last he called out,

»Ich hab's heraus!« Er ging mit ihm zu einer Quelle, 5.6
"I've found it!" He went with him to a spring,

5.7 tauchte sich hinein und kam als ein Marktkrämer und Tierhändler heraus.

dipped himself in and came out as a market trader and animal dealer.

5.8 Der Jüngling mußte sich auch in das Wasser tauchen und ward in ein kleines Meerhäschen verwandelt.

The young man also had to dip himself in the water and was transformed into a little mullet.

5.9 Der Kaufmann zog in die Stadt und zeigte das artige Tierchen.

The merchant went into the town and showed off the cute little animal.

5.10 Es lief viel Volk zusammen, um es anzusehen.

Many people came to see it.

5.11 Zuletzt kam auch die Königstochter, und weil sie großen Gefallen daran hatte, kaufte sie es und gab dem Kaufmann viel Geld dafür.

At last the king's daughter came too, and because she was very fond of it, she bought it and gave the merchant a lot of money for it.

5.12 Bevor er es ihr hinreichte, sagte er zu ihm,

Before he gave it to her, he said to him,

5.13 »Wenn die Königstochter ans Fenster geht,

"When the King's daughter goes to the window,

5.14 so krieche schnell unter ihren Zopf.«

crawl quickly under her braid."

5.15 Nun kam die Zeit, wo sie ihn suchen sollte.

Now the time came for her to look for him.

Sie trat nach der Reihe an die Fenster vom ersten bis zum elften und sah ihn nicht.   5.16

She went to the windows in order from the first to the eleventh and did not see him.

Als sie ihn auch bei dem zwölften nicht sah, war sie voll Angst und Zorn und schlug es so gewaltig zu, daß das Glas in allen Fenstern in tausend Stücke zersprang und das ganze Schloß erzitterte.   5.17

When she did not see him at the twelfth either, she was full of fear and rage, and she slammed it so violently that the glass in all the windows shattered into a thousand pieces and the whole castle trembled.

Sie ging zurück und fühlte das Meerhäschen unter ihrem Zopf, da packte sie es, warf es zu Boden und rief: 6.1

She went back and felt the mullet under her braid, so she grabbed it, threw it to the ground and shouted:

»Fort, mir aus den Augen!«   6.2

"Away, out of my sight!"

Es lief zum Kaufmann und beide eilten zur Quelle,   6.3

It ran to the merchant and both hurried to the spring,

wo sie sich untertauchten und ihre wahre Gestalt zurück erhielten.   6.4

where they immersed themselves and regained their true form.

Der Jüngling dankte dem Fuchs und sprach: 6.5

The young man thanked the fox and said:

6.6 »Der Rabe und der Fisch sind blitzdumm gegen dich,
du weißt die rechten Pfiffe, das muß wahr sein!«

"The raven and the fish are stupid as lightning against you,
you know the right whistles, that must be true!"

7.1 Der Jüngling ging geradezu in das Schloß.

The young man went straight into the castle.

7.2 Die Königstochter wartete schon auf ihn und fügte
sich ihrem Schicksal.

The king's daughter was already waiting for him and
resigned herself to her fate.

7.3 Die Hochzeit ward gefeiert und er war jetzt der König
und Herr des ganzen Reiches.

The wedding was celebrated and he was now king and lord
of the whole kingdom.

7.4 Er erzählte ihr niemals, wohin er sich zum
drittenmal versteckt und wer ihm geholfen hatte,
und so glaubte sie, er habe alles aus eigener Kunst
gethan und hatte Achtung vor ihm, denn sie dachte
bei sich,

He never told her where he had hidden himself for the
third time and who had helped him, and so she believed
that he had done everything by his own skill and had
respect for him, for she thought to herself,

7.5 »Der kann doch mehr als du!«

"He can do more than you!"

Der Meisterdieb

The Master Thief

1.1 **Eines Tages saß vor einem ärmlichen Hause ein alter Mann mit seiner Frau, und sie wollten von der Arbeit ein wenig ausruhen.**

One day, an old man and his wife were sitting outside a poor house, wanting to rest a little from their work.

1.2 **Da kam auf einmal ein prächtiger, mit vier Rappen bespannter Wagen herbeigefahren, aus dem ein reichgekleideter Herr stieg.**

Suddenly, a splendid wagon with four horses drove up and a richly dressed gentleman got out of it.

1.3 **Der Bauer stand auf, trat zu dem Herrn und fragte, was sein Verlangen wäre und worin er ihm dienen könnte.**

The farmer stood up, approached the gentleman and asked what he wanted and how he could serve him.

1.4 **Der Fremde reichte dem Alten die Hand und sagte:**

The stranger held out his hand to the old man and said:

1.5 **»Ich wünsche nichts als einmal ein ländliches Gericht zu genießen.**

"I want nothing more than to enjoy a country meal.

Bereitet mir Kartoffeln, wie Ihr sie zu essen pflegt, dann will ich mich zu Euerm Tisch setzen und sie mit Freude verzehren.«

1.6

Prepare me potatoes as you usually eat them, then I will sit down at your table and eat them with pleasure."

Der Bauer lächelte und sagte:

1.7

The farmer smiled and said,

»Ihr seid ein Graf oder Fürst, oder gar ein Herzog, vornehme Herren haben manchmal solch ein Gelüst;

1.8

"You are a count or a prince, or even a duke, noble gentlemen sometimes have such a desire;

Euer Wunsch soll aber erfüllt werden.«

1.9

but your wish shall be granted."

Die Frau ging in die Küche und sie fing an Kartoffeln zu waschen und zu reiben und wollte Klöße daraus bereiten,

1.10

The woman went into the kitchen and began to wash and grate potatoes and wanted to make dumplings out of them,

wie sie die Bauern essen. Während sie bei der Arbeit stand,

1.11

like the peasants eat. While she was working,

sagte der Bauer zu dem Fremden:

1.12

the farmer said to the stranger:

»Kommt einstweilen mit mir in meinen Hausgarten,

1.13

"Come with me into my garden,

wo ich noch etwas zu schaffen habe.«

1.14

where I still have some work to do."

1.15 In dem Garten hatte er Löcher gegraben und wollte jetzt Bäume einsetzen.

He had dug holes in the garden and now wanted to plant trees.

1.16 »Habt Ihr keine Kinder.« fragte der Fremde,

"Don't you have any children." asked the stranger,

1.17 »die Euch bei der Arbeit behilflich sein könnten?«

"who could help you with the work?"

1.18 »Nein.« antwortete der Bauer,

"No." replied the farmer,

1.19 »ich habe freilich einen Sohn gehabt.« setzte er hinzu,

"of course I had a son." he added,

1.20 »aber der ist schon seit langer Zeit in die weite Welt gegangen.

"but he left for the wide world a long time ago.

1.21 Es war ein ungeratener Junge, klug und verschlagen, aber er wollte nichts lernen und machte lauter böse Streiche;

He was an unadventurous boy, clever and cunning, but he didn't want to learn anything and was always up to mischief;

1.22 zuletzt lief er mir fort, und seitdem habe ich nichts von ihm gehört.«

at last he ran away and I haven't heard from him since."

1.23 Der Alte nahm ein Bäumchen,

The old man took a little tree,

1.24 setzte es in ein Loch und stieß einen Pfahl daneben;

put it in a hole and drove a stake beside it;

und als er Erde hineingeschaufelt und sie   1.25
festgestampft hatte, band er den Stamm unten, oben
und in der Mitte mit einem Strohseil fest an den
Pfahl.
and when he had shoveled earth into it and tamped it down,
he tied the trunk firmly to the stake at the bottom, top and
middle with a straw rope.

»Aber sagt mir.« sprach der Herr,   1.26
"But tell me." said the master,

»warum bindet Ihr den krummen knorrichten Baum,   1.27
der dort in der Ecke fast bis auf den Boden gebückt
liegt, nicht auch an einen Pfahl, wie diesen, damit er
strack wächst?«
"why don't you tie the crooked, gnarled tree lying there in
the corner, bent almost to the ground, to a stake like this
one, so that it grows straight?"

Der Alte lächelte und sagte: »Herr,   1.28
The old man smiled and said, "Sir,

Ihr redet wie Ihr's versteht;   1.29
you speak as you know how;

man sieht wohl, daß Ihr Euch mit der Gärtnerei nicht   1.30
abgegeben habt.
I can see that you have not bothered with gardening.

Der Baum dort ist alt und verknorzt,   1.31
That tree there is old and gnarled,

den kann niemand mehr gerade machen: 1.32
no one can straighten it:

Bäume muß man ziehen, so lange sie jung sind.«   1.33
One must pull trees while they are young."

1.34 »Es ist wie bei Eurem Sohn.« sagte der Fremde,
"It is like your son." said the stranger,

1.35 »hättet Ihr den gezogen wie er noch jung war,
"if you had pulled him when he was young,

1.36 so wäre er nicht fortgelaufen;
he would not have run away;

1.37 jetzt wird er auch hart und knorzig geworden sein.«
now he will also have become hard and gnarled."

1.38 »Freilich.« antwortete der Alte,
"Of course." replied the old man,

1.39 »es ist schon lange, seit er fortgegangen ist;
"it is a long time since he went away;

1.40 er wird sich verändert haben.«
he will have changed."

1.41 »Würdet Ihr ihn noch erkennen, wenn er vor Euch
träte?«
"Would you still recognize him if he stood before you?"

1.42 fragte der Fremde. »Am Gesicht schwerlich.«
asked the stranger. "Hardly by his face."

1.43 antwortete der Bauer,
replied the farmer,

1.44 »aber er hat ein Zeichen an sich, ein Muttermal auf
der Schulter, das wie eine Bohne aussieht.«
"but he has a mark on him, a birthmark on his shoulder
that looks like a bean."

Als er das gesagt hatte, zog der Fremde den Rock aus, entblößte seine Schulter und zeigte dem Bauer die Bohne. 1.45

When he had said this, the stranger took off his coat, bared his shoulder and showed the farmer the bean.

»Herr Gott.« rief der Alte, 1.46

"My God." exclaimed the old man,

»du bist wahrhaftig mein Sohn.« 1.47

"you are truly my son."

und die Liebe zu seinem Kinde regte sich in seinem Herzen. 1.48

and love for his child stirred in his heart.

»Aber.« setzte er hinzu, »wie kannst du mein Sohn sein, 1.49

"But." he added, "how can you be my son,

du bist ein großer Herr geworden und lebst in Reichtum und Überfluß? 1.50

you have become a great lord and live in wealth and abundance?

Auf welchem Wege bist du dazu gelangt?« 1.51

How did you get there?"

»Ach, Vater.« erwiderte der Sohn, 1.52

"Ah, father." replied the son,

»der junge Baum war an keinen Pfahl gebunden und ist krumm gewachsen; 1.53

"the young tree was not tied to a stake and grew crooked;

jetzt ist er zu alt; er wird nicht wieder gerade. 1.54

now it is too old; it will not grow straight again.

1.55 **Wie ich das alles erworben habe? Ich bin ein Dieb geworden.**
How did I get all this? I have become a thief.

1.56 **Aber erschreckt Euch nicht, ich bin ein Meisterdieb.**
But don't be frightened, I am a master thief.

1.57 **Für mich giebt es weder Schloß noch Riegel;**
For me there is neither lock nor bolt;

1.58 **wonach mich gelüstet, das ist mein.**
what I crave is mine.

1.59 **Glaubt nicht, daß ich stehle wie ein gemeiner Dieb, ich nehme nur vom Überfluß der Reichen.**
Do not think that I steal like a common thief, I only take from the abundance of the rich.

1.60 **Arme Leute sind sicher;**
Poor people are safe;

1.61 **ich gebe ihnen lieber, als daß ich ihnen etwas nehme.**
I would rather give them than take from them.

1.62 **So auch was ich ohne Mühe, List und Gewandtheit haben kann, das rühre ich nicht an.«**
Even what I can have without effort, cunning and skill, I do not touch."

1.63 **»Ach, mein Sohn.« sagte der Vater,**
"Ah, my son." said the father,

1.64 **»es gefällt mir doch nicht, ein Dieb bleibt ein Dieb;**
"I do not like it, a thief remains a thief;

1.65 **ich sage dir, es nimmt kein gutes Ende.«**
I tell you it will not end well."

Er führte ihn zu der Mutter, und als sie hörte, daß es ihr Sohn war, weinte sie vor Freude; 1.66
He took him to his mother, and when she heard that it was her son, she wept for joy;

als er ihr aber sagte, daß er ein Meisterdieb geworden wäre, so flossen ihr zwei Ströme über das Gesicht. 1.67
but when he told her that he had become a master thief, two rivers flowed down her face.

Endlich sagte sie: 1.68
At last she said,

»Wenn er auch ein Dieb geworden ist, so ist er doch mein Sohn, und meine Augen haben ihn noch einmal gesehen.« 1.69
"Though he has become a thief, yet he is my son, and my eyes have seen him once more."

Sie setzten sich an den Tisch und er aß mit seinen Eltern wieder einmal die schlechte Kost, die er lange nicht gegessen hatte. 2.1
They sat down at the table and he and his parents once again ate the bad food he had not eaten for a long time.

Der Vater sprach: 2.2
His father said,

2.3 »Wenn unser Herr, der Graf drüben im Schlosse, erfährt wer du bist und was du treibst, so nimmt er dich nicht auf die Arme und wiegt dich darin, wie er that, als er dich am Taufstein hielt, sondern er läßt dich am Galgenstrick schaukeln.«

"If our lord, the count over there in the castle, finds out who you are and what you are up to, he will not take you in his arms and cradle you in them, as he did when he held you at the baptismal font, but he will let you swing on the gallows rope."

2.4 »Seid ohne Sorge, mein Vater, er wird mir nichts thun, denn ich verstehe mein Handwerk.

"Don't worry, my father, he won't hurt me, for I know my trade.

2.5 Ich will heute noch selbst zu ihm gehen.«

I will go to him myself today."

2.6 Als die Abendzeit sich näherte,

As evening approached,

2.7 setzte sich der Meisterdieb in seinen Wagen und fuhr nach dem Schloß.

the master thief got into his carriage and drove to the castle.

2.8 Der Graf empfing ihn mit Artigkeit, weil er ihn für einen vornehmen Mann hielt.

The count received him with kindness because he considered him a gentleman.

2.9 Als aber der Fremde sich zu erkennen gab,

But when the stranger made himself known,

2.10 so erbleichte er und schwieg eine Zeitlang ganz still.

he turned pale and was silent for a while.

Endlich sprach er: »Du bist mein Pate,   2.11
At last he said, "You are my godfather,

deshalb will ich Gnade für Recht ergehen lassen und   2.12
nachsichtig mit dir verfahren.
so I will show you mercy and be lenient with you.

Weil du dich rühmst, ein Meisterdieb zu sein, so will   2.13
ich deine Kunst auf die Probe stellen;
As you boast of being a master thief, I will put your skill to
the test;

wenn du aber nicht bestehst, so mußt du mit des   2.14
Seilers Tochter Hochzeit halten und das Gekrächze
der Raben soll deine Musik dabei sein.«
but if you do not pass, you must marry the roper's daughter,
and the cawing of the ravens shall be your music."

»Herr Graf.« antwortete der Meister,   2.15
"Sir Count." replied the master,

»denkt Euch drei Stücke aus, so schwer Ihr wollt, und   2.16
wenn ich Eure Aufgabe nicht löse, so thut mit mir wie
Euch gefällt.«
"think of three pieces, as difficult as you like, and if I do not
solve your task, do with me as you please."

Der Graf sann einige Augenblicke nach, dann   2.17
sprach er:
The count pondered for a few moments, then he said,

2.18 »Wohlan, zum ersten sollst du mir mein Leibpferd aus dem Stalle stehlen, zum andern sollst du mir und meiner Gemahlin, wenn wir eingeschlafen sind, das Betttuch unter dem Leib wegnehmen, ohne daß wir's merken, und dazu meiner Gemahlin den Trauring vom Finger; zum dritten und letzten sollst du mir den Pfarrer und Küster aus der Kirche wegstehlen.

"Well, first, you shall steal my horse from the stable; secondly, you shall take the sheet from under me and my wife when we have fallen asleep, without our noticing it, and my wife's wedding ring from her finger; thirdly and lastly, you shall steal the priest and sexton from the church.

2.19 Merke dir alles wohl, denn es geht dir an den Hals.«

Remember all this well, for it will be your neck."

3.1 Der Meister begab sich in die zunächst liegende Stadt.

The master went to the town next door.

3.2 Dort kaufte er einer alten Bauernfrau die Kleider ab und zog sie an.

There he bought clothes from an old peasant woman and put them on.

3.3 Dann färbte er sich das Gesicht braun und malte sich noch Runzeln hinein, sodaß ihn kein Mensch wiedererkannt hätte.

Then he dyed his face brown and painted wrinkles into it so that no one would have recognized him.

3.4 Endlich füllte er ein Fäßchen mit altem Ungarwein in welchen ein starker Schlaftrunk gemischt war.

At last he filled a small cask with old Hungarian wine mixed with a strong sleeping draught.

Das Fäßchen legte er auf eine Kötze, die er auf
den Rücken nahm, und ging mit bedächtigen,
schwankenden Schritten zu dem Schloß des Grafen. 3.5
He placed the cask on his back and walked with deliberate,
swaying steps to the count's castle.

Es war schon dunkel, als er anlangte; 3.6
It was already dark when he arrived;

er setzte sich in dem Hofe auf einen Stein, fing an zu 3.7
husten wie eine alte brustkranke Frau und rieb die
Hände, als wenn er fröre.
he sat down on a stone in the courtyard, began to cough
like an old woman with a chest disease, and rubbed his
hands as if he were convalescing.

Vor der Thür des Pferdestalles lagen Soldaten um ein 3.8
Feuer;
Soldiers were lying around a fire at the door of the stable;

einer von ihnen bemerkte die Frau und rief ihr zu: 3.9
one of them noticed the woman and called out to her:

»Komm näher, altes Mütterchen, und wärme dich bei 3.10
uns.
"Come closer, old mother, and warm yourself with us.

Du hast doch kein Nachtlager und nimmst es an, wo 3.11
du es findest.«
You don't have a place to stay for the night and take it
where you find it."

Die Alte trippelte herbei, bat, ihr die Kötze vom 3.12
Rücken zu heben, und setzte sich zu ihnen ans Feuer.
The old woman trundled over, asked them to lift her head
off her back and sat down by the fire.

3.13 »Was hast du da in deinem Fäßchen, du alte Schachtel?«
"What have you got in your little barrel, you old hag?"

3.14 fragte einer. »Einen guten Schluck Wein.« antwortete sie,
asked one of them. "A good glass of wine." she replied,

3.15 »ich ernähre mich mit dem Handel,
"I make my living by trading,

3.16 für Geld und gute Worte gebe ich Euch gern ein Glas.«
and I'll gladly give you a glass for money and good words."

3.17 »Nur her damit.«
"Give it to me."

3.18 sagte der Soldat, und als er ein Glas gekostet hatte, rief er:
said the soldier, and when he had tasted a glass, he exclaimed,

3.19 »Wenn der Wein gut ist, so trink ich lieber ein Glas mehr.«
"If the wine is good, I'd rather drink a glass more."

3.20 ließ sich nochmals einschenken, und die anderen folgten seinem Beispiel.
He poured himself another glass and the others followed his example.

3.21 »Heda, Kameraden.«
"Heda, comrades."

3.22 rief einer denen zu, die in dem Stalle saßen,
one of them called to those sitting in the stable,

»hier ist ein Mütterchen, das hat Wein, der so alt ist wie sie selber, nehmt auch einen Schluck, der wärmt euch den Magen noch besser als unser Feuer.« 3.23

"here is a little mother who has wine as old as herself, take a sip, it will warm your stomachs even better than our fire."

Die Alte trug ihr Fäßchen in den Stall. 3.24

The old woman carried her cask into the stable.

Einer hatte sich auf das gesattelte Leibpferd gesetzt, ein anderer hielt den Zaum in der Hand, ein dritter hatte den Schwanz gepackt. 3.25

One of them had sat on the saddled horse, another held the bridle in his hand and a third had grabbed the tail.

Sie schenkte ein, so viel verlangt ward, bis die Quelle versiegte. 3.26

They poured as much as they wanted until the spring ran dry.

Nicht lange, so fiel dem einen der Zaum aus der Hand, er sank nieder und fing an zu schnarchen, der andere ließ den Schwanz los, legte sich nieder und schnarchte noch lauter. 3.27

Before long, the bridle fell from the hand of one of them, he sank down and began to snore, the other let go of the tail, lay down and snored even louder.

Der, welcher im Sattel saß, blieb zwar sitzen, bog sich aber mit dem Kopf fast bis auf den Hals des Pferdes, schlief und blies mit dem Munde wie ein Schmiedebalg. 3.28

The one in the saddle remained seated, but bent his head almost to the horse's neck, slept and blew with his mouth like a blacksmith's bellows.

3.29 Die Soldaten draußen waren schon längst eingeschlafen, lagen auf der Erde und regten sich nicht, als wären sie von Stein.

The soldiers outside had long since fallen asleep, lying on the ground and not moving as if they were made of stone.

3.30 Als der Meisterdieb sah, daß es ihm geglückt war, gab er dem einen statt des Zaums ein Seil in die Hand und dem anderen, der den Schwanz gehalten hatte, einen Strohwisch;

When the master thief saw that he had succeeded, he gave one of them a rope instead of the bridle, and the other, who had been holding the tail, a straw mop;

3.31 aber was sollte er mit dem, der auf dem Rücken des Pferdes saß, anfangen?

but what was he to do with the one on the horse's back?

3.32 Herunterwerfen wollte er ihn nicht, er hätte erwachen und ein Geschrei erheben können.

He didn't want to throw him down; he might have woken up and raised a cry.

3.33 Er wußte aber guten Rat, er schnallte den Sattelgurt auf, knüpfte ein paar Seile, die in Ringen an der Wand hingen, an den Sattel fest, und zog den schlafenden Reiter mit dem Sattel in die Höhe, dann schlug er die Seile um den Pfosten und machte sie fest.

But he knew good advice, he unbuckled the saddle girth, tied a few ropes hanging in rings on the wall to the saddle and pulled the sleeping rider up with the saddle, then he looped the ropes around the post and fastened them.

3.34 Das Pferd hatte er bald von der Kette losgebunden;

He soon had the horse untied from the chain;

aber wenn er über das steinerne Pflaster des Hofes geritten wäre,   3.35
but if he had ridden over the stone pavement of the courtyard,

so hätte man den Lärm im Schlosse gehört.   3.36
the noise would have been heard in the castle.

Er umwickelte ihm also zuvor die Hufen mit alten Lappen, führte es dann vorsichtig hinaus, schwang sich auf und jagte davon.   3.37
So he first wrapped old rags around its hooves, then carefully led it out, swung himself up and chased off.

Als der Tag angebrochen war,   4.1
When day broke,

sprengte der Meister auf dem gestohlenen Pferd zu dem Schloß.   4.2
the master rode up to the castle on the stolen horse.

Der Graf war eben aufgestanden und blickte aus dem Fenster.   4.3
The count had just got up and was looking out of the window.

»Guten Morgen, Herr Graf.« rief er ihm zu,   4.4
"Good morning, Count." he called to him,

»hier ist das Pferd, das ich glücklich aus dem Stall geholt habe.   4.5
"here is the horse I happily got out of the stable.

4.6 Schaut nur, wie schön Eure Soldaten da liegen und schlafen, und wenn Ihr in den Stall gehen wollt, so werdet Ihr sehen, wie bequem sich's Eure Wächter gemacht haben.«

Look how nicely your soldiers are lying there and sleeping, and if you will go into the stable, you will see how comfortable your guards have made themselves."

4.7 Der Graf mußte lachen, dann sprach er,

The count had to laugh, then he said,

4.8 »Einmal ist dir's gelungen,

"You succeeded once,

4.9 aber das zweite Mal wird's nichts so glücklich ablaufen.

but the second time it won't go so well.

4.10 Und ich warne dich, wenn du mir als Dieb begegnest, so behandle ich dich auch wie ein Dieb.«

And I warn you, if you meet me as a thief, I will treat you as a thief."

4.11 Als die Gräfin abends zu Bette gegangen war, schloß sie die Hand mit dem Trauring fest zu, und der Graf sagte,

When the countess had gone to bed at night, she closed her hand tightly with the wedding-ring, and the count said,

4.12 »Alle Thüren sind verschlossen und verriegelt,

"All the doors are locked and bolted,

4.13 ich bleibe wach und will den Dieb erwarten;

I will stay awake and await the thief;

4.14 steigt er aber zum Fenster ein, so schieße ich ihn nieder.«

but if he gets in at the window, I will shoot him down."

Der Meisterdieb aber ging in der Dunkelheit hinaus   4.15
zu dem Galgen, schnitt einen armen Sünder, der da
hing, von dem Strick ab und trug ihn auf dem Rücken
nach dem Schloß.
But the master thief went out in the darkness to the
gallows, cut off the rope from a poor sinner who was
hanging there, and carried him on his back to the castle.

Dort stellte er eine Leiter an das Schlafgemach,   4.16
There he placed a ladder by the bedchamber,

setzte den Toten auf seine Schultern und fing an   4.17
hinauf zu steigen.
put the dead man on his shoulders and began to climb up.

Als er so hoch gekommen war, daß der Kopf des   4.18
Toten in dem Fenster erschien, drückte der Graf, der
in seinem Bett lauerte, eine Pistole auf ihn los:
When he had got so high that the dead man's head
appeared in the window, the count, who was lurking in
his bed, discharged a pistol at him:

alsbald ließ der Meister den armen Sünder   4.19
herabfallen, sprang selbst die Leiter herab, und
versteckte sich in eine Ecke.
immediately the master let the poor sinner fall down,
jumped down the ladder himself, and hid himself in a
corner.

Die Nacht war von dem Mond so weit erhellt, daß der   4.20
Meister deutlich sehen konnte wie der Graf aus dem
Fenster auf die Leiter stieg, herabkam und den Toten
in den Garten trug.
The night was so well lit by the moon that the master could
see clearly how the count climbed down the ladder from
the window, came down and carried the dead man into the
garden.

4.21 Dort fing er an ein Loch zu graben, in das er ihn legen wollte.

There he began to dig a hole in which to lay him.

4.22 »Jetzt.« dachte der Dieb,

"Now." thought the thief,

4.23 »ist der günstige Augenblick gekommen.«

"the opportune moment has come."

4.24 schlich behende aus seinem Winkel und stieg die Leiter hinauf,

He crept nimbly out of his corner and climbed up the ladder,

4.25 geradezu ins Schlafgemach der Gräfin. »Liebe Frau.«

straight into the countess's bedchamber. "My dear lady."

4.26 fing er mit der Stimme des Grafen an,

he began, in the count's voice,

4.27 »der Dieb ist tot, aber er ist doch mein Pate und mehr ein Schelm als ein Bösewicht gewesen; ich will ihn der öffentlichen Schande nicht preisgeben; auch mit den armen Eltern habe ich Mitleid.

"the thief is dead, but he is my godfather, and was more of a rogue than a villain; I will not expose him to public disgrace, and I pity his poor parents.

4.28 Ich will ihn, bevor der Tag anbricht, selbst im Garten begraben, damit die Sache nicht ruchbar wird.

I will bury him myself in the garden before the day dawns, so that the matter will not become notorious.

4.29 Gieb mir auch das Betttuch, so will ich die Leiche einhüllen und ihn wie einen Hund verscharren.«

Give me the sheet, too, and I will wrap up the body and bury him like a dog."

Die Gräfin gab ihm das Tuch. »Weißt du was.«   4.30
The countess gave him the sheet. "You know what."

sagte der Dieb weiter,   4.31
said the thief,

»ich habe eine Anwandlung von Großmut, gieb mir   4.32
noch den Ring;
"I have a touch of magnanimity, give me the ring;

der Unglückliche hat sein Leben gewagt,   4.33
the unfortunate man has dared to live,

so mag er ihn ins Grab mitnehmen.«   4.34
so let him take it with him to the grave."

Sie wollte dem Grafen nicht entgegen sein, und   4.35
obgleich sie es ungern that, so zog sie doch den Ring
vom Finger und reichte ihn hin.
She did not want to oppose the count, and although she
was reluctant to do so, she took the ring off her finger and
handed it over.

Der Dieb machte sich mit beiden Stücken fort und   4.36
kam glücklich nach.
The thief made off with both pieces and returned home
happily.

Hause, bevor der Graf im Garten mit seiner   4.37
Totengräberarbeit fertig war.
He was home before the count had finished his grave-
digging in the garden.

Was zog der Graf für ein langes Gesicht, als am   5.1
anderen.
What a long face the count pulled when the master came
the next morning and brought him the sheet and the ring.

5.2 Morgen der Meister kam und ihm das Betttuch und den Ring brachte.

In the morning the master came and brought him the sheet and the ring.

5.3 »Kannst du hexen?« sagte er zu ihm,

"Can you do witchcraft?" he said to him,

5.4 »wer hat dich aus dem Grabe geholt, in das ich selbst dich gelegt habe, und hat dich wieder lebendig gemacht?«

"who took you out of the grave in which I myself laid you and brought you back to life?"

5.5 »Mich habt Ihr nicht begraben.« sagte der Dieb,

"You did not bury me." said the thief,

5.6 »sondern den armen Sünder am Galgen.«

"but the poor sinner on the gallows."

5.7 und erzählte ausführlich wie es zugegangen war;

and told him in detail how it had happened;

5.8 und der Graf mußte ihm zugestehen, daß er ein gescheiter und listiger Dieb wäre.

and the count had to admit to him that he was a clever and cunning thief.

5.9 »Aber noch bist du nicht zu Ende.« setzte er hinzu,

"But you're not finished yet." he added,

5.10 »du hast noch die dritte Aufgabe zu lösen und wenn dir das nicht gelingt, so hilft dir alles nichts.«

"you still have the third task to solve, and if you don't succeed, nothing will help you."

Der Meister lächelte und gab keine Antwort.   5.11

The master smiled and made no reply.

Als die Nacht angebrochen war, kam er mit einem   6.1
langen Sack auf dem Rücken, einem Bündel unter
dem Arm und einer Laterne in der Hand zu der
Dorfkirche gegangen.

When night had fallen, he came to the village church with a
long sack on his back, a bundle under his arm and a lantern
in his hand.

In dem Sack hatte er Krebse, in dem Bündel aber   6.2
kurze Wachslichter. ᷄

He had crabs in the sack and short wax candles in the
bundle.

Er setzte sich auf den Gottesacker, holte einen Krebs   6.3
heraus und klebte ihm ein Wachslichtchen auf den
Rücken, dann zündete er das Lichtchen an, setzte den
Krebs auf den Boden und ließ ihn kriechen.

He sat down in the churchyard, took out a crab and stuck a
wax light on its back, then lit the light, put the crab on the
ground and let it crawl.

Er holte einen zweiten aus dem Sack, machte es mit   6.4
diesem ebenso und fuhr fort, bis auch der letzte aus
dem Sacke war.

He took a second one out of the bag, did the same with this
one and continued until the last one was out of the bag.

Hierauf zog er ein langes schwarzes Gewand an, das   6.5
wie eine Mönchskutte aussah und klebte sich einen
grauen Bart an das Kinn.

Then he put on a long black robe that looked like a monk's
habit and stuck a gray beard on his chin.

6.6 Als er endlich ganz unkenntlich war, nahm er den Sack, in dem die Krebse gewesen waren, ging in die Kirche und stieg auf die Kanzel.

When he was finally completely unrecognizable, he took the sack in which the crabs had been, went into the church and climbed into the pulpit.

6.7 Die Turmuhr schlug eben zwölf:

The tower clock was just striking twelve:

6.8 als der letzte Schlag verklungen war, rief er mit lauter, gellender Stimme:

when the last stroke had died away, he called out in a loud, resounding voice:

6.9 »Hört an, ihr sündigen Menschen, das Ende aller Dinge ist gekommen, der jüngste Tag ist nahe:

"Listen, you sinful people, the end of all things has come, the last day is near:

6.10 hört an! hört an! Wer mit mir in den Himmel will,

listen! listen! Whoever wants to go to heaven with me,

6.11 der krieche in den Sack. Ich bin Petrus,

let him crawl into the sack. I am Peter,

6.12 der die Himmelsthür öffnet und schließt. Seht ihr,

who opens and closes the door of heaven. You see,

6.13 draußen auf dem Gottesacker wandeln die Gestorbenen und sammeln ihre Gebeine zusammen.

outside on God's field the dead walk and gather their bones together.

6.14 Kommt, kommt und kriecht in den Sack, die Welt geht unter.«

Come, come and crawl into the sack, the world is coming to an end."

Das Geschrei erschallte durch das ganze Dorf. 6.15

The cry resounded throughout the village.

Der Pfarrer und der Küster, die zunächst an der 6.16
Kirche wohnten hatten es zuerst vernommen,
und als sie die Lichter erblickten, die auf dem
Gottesacker umherwandelten, merkten sie, daß
etwas Ungewöhnliches vorging und traten in die
Kirche ein.

The priest and the sexton, who lived next to the church,
heard it first, and when they saw the lights wandering
around the churchyard, they realized that something
unusual was going on and entered the church.

Sie hörten der Predigt eine Weile zu, da stieß der 6.17
Küster den Pfarrer an und sprach:

They listened to the sermon for a while, when the sexton
nudged the priest and said,

»Es wäre nicht übel, wenn wir die Gelegenheit 6.18
benutzten und zusammen vor dem Anbruch des
jüngsten Tages auf eine leichte Art in den Himmel
kämen.«

"It wouldn't be bad if we took the opportunity and went to
heaven together in a light way before the dawn of the last
day."

»Freilich.« erwiderte der Pfarrer, 6.19

"Of course." replied the priest,

»das sind auch meine Gedanken gewesen; habt Ihr 6.20
Lust,

"those were my thoughts too; if you feel like it,

so wollen wir uns auf den Weg machen.« 6.21

let's set off."

6.22 »Ja.« antwortete der Küster,
"Yes." replied the sexton,

6.23 »aber Ihr, Herr Pfarrer, habt den Vortritt, ich folge nach.«
"but you, Father, have the right of way, I will follow."

6.24 Der Pfarrer schritt also vor und stieg auf die Kanzel,
So the priest went ahead and climbed up to the pulpit,

6.25 wo der Meister den Sack öffnete.
where the master opened the sack.

6.26 Der Pfarrer kroch zuerst hinein, »dann der Küster.
The priest crawled in first, "then the sexton.

6.27 Gleich band der Meister den Sack fest zu,
Immediately the master tied the sack tightly,

6.28 packte ihn am Bausch und schleifte ihn die Kanzeltreppe hinab;
grabbed it by the pouch and dragged it down the pulpit stairs;

6.29 so oft die Köpfe der beiden Thoren auf die Stufen aufschlugen,
as often as the heads of the two doors hit the steps,

6.30 rief er: »Jetzt geht's schon über die Berge.«
he shouted: "Now it's already over the mountains."

6.31 Dann zog er sie auf gleiche Weise durch das Dorf, und wenn sie durch Pfützen kamen, rief er,
Then he pulled them through the village in the same way, and when they came through puddles, he called out,

»Jetzt geht's schon durch die nassen Wolken.«   6.32
"Now we're going through the wet clouds."

und als er sie endlich die Schloßtreppe hinaufzog, so   6.33
rief er:
And when he finally pulled them up the castle steps, he
called out,

»Jetzt sind wir auf der Himmelstreppe und werden   6.34
bald im Vorhof sein.«
"Now we're on the stairway to heaven and will soon be in
the forecourt."

Als er oben angelangt war, schob er den Sack in   6.35
den Taubenschlag, und als die Tauben flatterten,
sagte er:
When he had reached the top, he pushed the sack into the
dovecote, and as the doves fluttered, he said,

»Hört ihr, wie die Engel sich freuen und mit den   6.36
Fittichen schlagen.«
"Hear how the angels rejoice and flap their wings."

Dann schob er den Riegel vor und ging fort.   6.37
Then he pushed the latch forward and left.

Am anderen Morgen begab er sich zu dem Grafen und   7.1
sagte ihm, daß er auch die dritte Aufgabe gelöst und
den Pfarrer und Küster, aus der Kirche weggeführt
hätte.
The next morning he went to the count and told him that he
had also completed the third task and had led the priest and
sexton out of the church.

»Wo hast du sie gelassen?« fragte der Herr.   7.2
"Where have you left them?" asked the lord.

7.3 »Sie liegen in einem Sack oben aus dem Taubenschlag und bilden sich ein,

"They are lying in a sack at the top of the dovecote,

7.4 sie wären im Himmel.«

imagining they are in heaven."

7.5 Der Graf stieg selbst hinauf und überzeugte sich, daß er die Wahrheit gesagt hatte.

The count went up himself and convinced himself that he had told the truth.

7.6 Als, er den Pfarrer und Küster aus dem Gefängnis befreit hatte, sprach er:

When he had freed the priest and sexton from prison, he said:

7.7 »Du bist ein Erzdieb und hast deine Sache gewonnen.

"You are an arch-thief and have won your case.

7.8 Für diesmal kommst du mit heiler Haut davon, aber mache, daß du aus, meinem Lande fortkommst, denn wenn du dich wieder darin betreten läßt, so kannst du auf deine Erhöhung am Galgen rechnen.«

For this time you will get off with your skin intact, but make sure you get out of my country, for if you allow yourself to enter it again, you can expect to be hanged."

7.9 Der Erzdieb nahm Abschied von seinen Eltern, ging wieder in die weite Welt und niemand hat wieder etwas von ihm gehört.

The arch-thief took leave of his parents, went into the wide world again, and no one ever heard of him again.

Der Trommler

The Drummer

1.1 **Eines Abends ging ein junger Trommler ganz allein auf dem Feld und kam an einen See, da sah er an dem Ufer drei Stückchen weiße Leinwand liegen,**
One evening, a young drummer was walking alone in the fields and came to a lake, where he saw three pieces of white canvas lying on the shore,

1.2 **»Was für feines Leinen.«**
"What fine linen."

1.3 **sprach er und steckte eins davon in die Tasche. Er ging heim,**
he said and put one of them in his pocket. He went home,

1.4 **dachte nicht weiter an seinen Fund und legte sich zu Bett.**
thought nothing more of his find and went to bed.

1.5 **Als er eben einschlafen wollte, war es ihm, als nenne jemand seinen Namen.**
As he was about to fall asleep, he felt as if someone was calling his name.

Er horchte, und vernahm eine leise Stimme, die ihm zurief:

1.6

He listened and heard a soft voice calling out to him:

»Trommler, Trommler, wach auf.«

1.7

"Drummer, drummer, wake up."

Er konnte, da es finstere.

1.8

It was dark and he couldn't see anyone.

Nacht war, niemand sehen, aber es kam ihm vor als schwebte eine Gestalt vor seinem Bett, auf und ab.

1.9

night, he couldn't see anyone, but it seemed to him that a figure was floating up and down in front of his bed.

»Was willst du?« fragte er.

1.10

"What do you want?" he asked.

»Gieb mir mein Hemdchen zurück.« antwortete die Stimme,

1.11

"Give me back my shirt." the voice replied,

»das du mir gestern abend am See weggenommen hast.«

1.12

"the one you took from me last night at the lake."

»Du sollst es wieder haben.« sprach der Trommler,

1.13

"You shall have it back." said the drummer,

»wenn du mir sagst, wer du bist.«

1.14

"if you tell me who you are."

»Ach.« erwiderte die Stimme,

1.15

"Ah." replied the voice,

1.16 »ich bin die Tochter eines mächtigen Königs, aber ich bin in, die Gewalt einer Hexe geraten, und bin auf den Glasberg gebannt.

"I am the daughter of a mighty king, but I have fallen into the power of a witch, and am banished to the glass mountain.

1.17 Jeden Tag muß ich mich mit meinen zwei Schwestern im See baden,

Every day I have to bathe in the lake with my two sisters,

1.18 aber ohne mein Hemdchen kann ich nicht wieder fortfliegen.

but I can't fly away again without my little shirt.

1.19 Meine Schwestern haben sich, fortgemacht, ich aber habe zurückbleiben müssen.

My sisters have gone away, but I have had to stay behind.

1.20 Ich bitte dich, gieb mir mein Hemdchen wieder.«

I beg you to give me back my shirt."

1.21 »Sei ruhig, armes Kind.« sprach, der Trommler,

"Be quiet, poor child." said the drummer,

1.22 »ich will dir's gern zurückgehen.«

"I will gladly give it back to you."

1.23 Er holte es aus seiner Tasche und reichte es ihr in der Dunkelheit hin.

He took it out of his pocket and handed it to her in the darkness.

1.24 Sie erfaßte es hastig und wollte damit fort.

She seized it hastily and wanted to go away with it.

1.25 »Weile einen Augenblick.« sagte er,

"Wait a moment." he said,

»vielleicht kann ich dir helfen.«   1.26
"perhaps I can help you."

»Helfen kannst du mir nur, wenn du auf den Glasberg   1.27
steigst und mich, aus der Gewalt der Hexe befreist.
"You can only help me if you climb the glass mountain and
free me from the witch's control.

Aber zu dem Glasberg kommst, du nicht, und wenn   1.28
du auch ganz nahe daran, wärst, so kommst du nicht
hinauf.«
But you won't get to the glass mountain, and even if you
were very close to it, you won't get up there."

»Was ich will, das kann ich.« sagte der Trommler,   1.29
"I can do what I want." said the drummer,

»ich habe Mitleid mit dir und ich fürchte mich vor   1.30
nichts.
"I have pity on you and I'm not afraid of anything.

Aber ich weiß den Weg nicht, der nach dem   1.31
Glasberge führt.«
But I don't know the way that leads to the Glass Mountain."

»Der Weg geht durch den großen Wald, in dem die   1.32
Menschenfresser hausen.«
"The path goes through the great forest where the man-
eaters live."

antwortete sie, »mehr darf ich dir nicht sagen.«   1.33
she replied, "I must not tell you more."

Darauf hörte er wie sie fortschwirrte.   1.34
Then he heard her whizz away.

2.1 Bei Anbruch des, Tages, machte, sich der Trommler auf, hing seine Trommel um und ging, ohne Furcht geradezu in den Wald hinein.

At dawn, the drummer got up, hung up his drum and went straight into the forest without fear.

2.2 Als er ein Weilchen gegangen war und keinen Riesen erblickte, so dachte, er:

When he had walked for a while and saw no giant, he thought:

2.3 »Ich, muß die Langschläfer aufwecken.«

"I must wake up the late risers."

2.4 hing die Trommel, vor und schlug einen Wirbel, daß die Vögel aus den Bäumen mit Geschrei aufflogen.

He hung the drum in front of him and beat it so loudly that the birds flew up from the trees with a cry.

2.5 Nicht lange so erhob sich auch ein Riese in die Höhe, der im Gras gelegen und geschlafen hatte, und war so groß wie eine Tanne.

It was not long before a giant, who had been lying in the grass and sleeping, rose into the air and was as big as a fir-tree.

2.6 »Du Wicht.« rief er ihm zu,

"You wretch." he called to him,

2.7 »was trommelst du hier und weckst mich aus dem besten Schlaf?«

"what are you drumming here and waking me from my sound sleep?"

2.8 »Ich trommle.« antwortete er,

"I am drumming." he replied,

»weil viele Tausende hinter mir herkommen, damit sie den Weg wissen.« 2.9

"because many thousands are coming after me so that they know the way."

»Was wollen die hier in meinem Wald?« fragte der Riese. 2.10

"What do they want here in my forest?" asked the giant.

»Sie wollen dir den Garaus machen und den Wald von einem Ungetüm, wie du bist, säubern.« 2.11

"They want to finish you off and clear the forest of a monster like you."

»Oho.« sagte der Riese, »ich trete euch wie Ameisen tot.« 2.12

"Oho." said the giant, "I'll kick you to death like ants."

»Meinst du, du könntest gegen sie etwas ausrichten?« 2.13

"Do you think you could do anything against them?"

sprach der Trommler, 2.14

said the drummer,

»wenn du dich bückst, um einen zu packen, so springt er fort und versteckt sich; 2.15

"if you bend down to seize one, he jumps away and hides;

wie du dich aber niederlegst und schläfst, 2.16

but as you lie down and sleep,

so kommen sie aus allen Gebüschen herbei und kriechen an dir hinauf. 2.17

they come out of all the bushes and crawl up to you.

2.18 Jeder hat einen Hammer von Stahl am Gürtel stecken,
Each has a hammer of steel stuck to his belt,

2.19 damit schlagen sie dir den Schädel ein.«
with which they smash your skull."

2.20 Der Riese ward verdrießlich und dachte:
The giant became annoyed and thought:

2.21 »Wenn ich mich mit dem listigen Volk befasse,
"If I deal with the cunning people,

2.22 so könnte es doch zu meinem Schaden ausschlagen.
it could turn out to my disadvantage.

2.23 Wölfen und Bären drücke ich die Gurgel zusammen,
I can squeeze the throats of wolves and bears,

2.24 aber vor den Erdwürmern kann ich mich nicht schützen.«
but I can't protect myself from earthworms."

2.25 »Hör, kleiner Kerl.« sprach er,
"Listen, little fellow." said he,

2.26 »zieh wieder ab, ich verspreche dir, daß ich dich und deine Gesellen in Zukunft in Ruhe lasten will, und hast du noch einen Wunsch, so sag's mir, ich will dir wohl etwas zu Gefallen thun.«
"go away again, I promise you that I will leave you and your companions in peace in future, and if you have another wish, tell me, and I will do you a favor."

2.27 »Du hast lange Beine.« sprach der Trommler,
"Thou hast long legs." said the drummer,

»und kannst schneller laufen als ich, trag mich zum Glasberge, so will ich den Meinigen ein Zeichen zum Rückzug geben und sie sollen dich diesmal in Ruhe lassen.«

2.28

"and canst run faster than I can; carry me to the glass mountain, and I will give my own a signal to retreat, and they shall leave thee alone this time."

»Komm her, Wurm.« sprach der Riese,

2.29

"Come here, worm." said the giant,

»setz dich auf meine Schulter,

2.30

"sit on my shoulder,

ich will dich tragen wohin du verlangst.«

2.31

I will carry you wherever you wish."

Der Riese hob ihn hinauf, und der Trommler fing oben an nach Herzenslust auf der Trommel zu wirbeln.

2.32

The giant lifted him up and the drummer began to twirl the drum to his heart's content.

Der Riese dachte:

2.33

The giant thought:

»Das wird das Zeichen sein, daß das andere Volk zurückgehen soll.«

2.34

"That will be the sign that the other people should go back."

Nach einer Weile stand ein zweiter Riese am Wege,

2.35

After a while a second giant stood by the road,

der nahm den Trommler dem ersten ab und steckte ihn in sein Knopfloch.

2.36

who took the drummer from the first and put him in his buttonhole.

2.37 Der Trommler faßte den Knopf, der wie eine Schüssel groß war, hielt sich daran und schaute ganz lustig umher.

The drummer took hold of the button, which was the size of a bowl, held on to it, and looked about with great amusement.

2.38 Dann kamen sie zu einem dritten, der nahm ihn aus dem Knopfloch und setzte ihn auf den Rand seines Hutes: da ging der Trommler oben auf und ab und sah über die Bäume hinaus, und als er in blauer Ferne einen Berg erblickte, so dachte er,

Then they came to a third, who took it out of his buttonhole and put it on the brim of his hat, and the drummer walked up and down and looked out over the trees, and when he saw a mountain in the blue distance, he thought,

2.39 »Das ist gewiß der Glasberg.« und er war es auch.

"That is certainly the Glass Mountain." and it was.

2.40 Der Riese that nur noch ein paar Schritte, so wären sie an dem Fuß des Berges angelangt, wo ihn der Riese absetzte.

The giant only took a few more steps and they would have reached the foot of the mountain, where the giant set him down.

2.41 Der Trommler verlangte, er sollte ihn auch auf die Spitze des Glasberges tragen, aber der Riese schüttelte mit dem Kopfe, brummte etwas in den Bart und ging in den Wald zurück.

The drummer demanded that he should also carry him to the top of the Glass Mountain, but the giant shook his head, mumbled something into his beard and went back into the forest.

Nun stand der arme Trommler vor dem Berge, der so hoch war, als wenn drei Berge aufeinander gesetzt wären, und dabei so glatt wie ein Spiegel, und wußte keinen Rat, um hinauf zu kommen. **3.1**

Now the poor drummer stood in front of the mountain, which was as high as if three mountains had been placed on top of each other, and as smooth as a mirror, and knew no way to get up.

Er fing an zu klettern, aber vergeblich, er rutschte immer wieder herab. **3.2**

He began to climb, but in vain; he kept slipping down.

»Wer jetzt ein Vogel wäre.« **3.3**

"Who would be a bird now."

dachte er, aber was half das Wünschen, es wuchsen ihm keine Flügel. **3.4**

he thought, but what was the use of wishing, he grew no wings.

Indem er so stand und sich nicht zu helfen wußte, erblickte er nicht weit von sich zwei Männer, die heftig miteinander stritten. **3.5**

As he stood there, unable to help himself, he saw two men not far from him, arguing violently with each other.

Er ging auf sie zu und sah, daß sie wegen eines Sattels uneins waren, der vor ihnen auf der Erde lag und den jeder von ihnen haben wollte. **3.6**

He approached them and saw that they were at odds over a saddle lying on the ground in front of them, which each of them wanted.

»Was seid ihr für Narren.« sprach er, **3.7**

"What fools you are." said he,

3.8 »zankt euch um einen Sattel und habt kein Pferd dazu.«
"quarrelling about a saddle and having no horse for it."

3.9 »Der Sattel ist wert, daß man darum streitet.«
"The saddle is worth quarrelling over."

3.10 antwortete der eine von den Männern,
answered one of the men,

3.11 »wer darauf sitzt und wünscht sich irgendwohin, und wär's am Ende der Welt, der ist im Augenblick angelangt, wie er den Wunsch ausgesprochen hat.
"whoever sits on it and wishes to go anywhere, even to the end of the world, has arrived at the moment he has expressed his wish.

3.12 Der Sattel gehört uns gemeinschaftlich, die Reihe darauf zu reiten ist an mir, aber der andere will es nicht zulassen.«
The saddle belongs to us jointly, it's my turn to ride on it, but the other one won't let me."

3.13 »Den Streit will ich bald austragen.« sagte der Trommler,
"I will settle the dispute soon." said the drummer,

3.14 ging eine Strecke weit und steckte einen weißen Stab in die Erde.
walked a distance and stuck a white stick into the ground.

3.15 Dann kam er zurück und sprach:
Then he came back and said:

3.16 »Jetzt lauft nach dem Ziel, wer zuerst dort ist, der reitet zuerst.«
"Now run to the finish, whoever gets there first rides first."

Beide setzten sich in Trab, aber kaum waren sie ein paar Schritte weg, so schwang sich der Trommler auf den Sattel, wünschte sich auf den Glasberg, und ehe man die Hand umdrehte, war er dort.   3.17

They both set off at a trot, but as soon as they were a few steps away, the drummer swung himself onto the saddle, wished himself onto the glass mountain, and before you could turn your hand around, he was there.

Auf dem Berge oben war eine Ebene, da stand ein altes steinernes Haus, und vor dem Hause lag ein großer Fischteich, dahinter aber ein finsterer Wald.   3.18

There was a plain at the top of the mountain, where an old stone house stood, and in front of the house was a large fishpond, but behind it was a dark forest.

Menschen und Tiere sah er nicht, es war alles still, nur der Wind raschelte in den Bäumen, und die Wolken zogen ganz nahe über seinem Haupt weg.   3.19

He did not see any people or animals, everything was quiet, only the wind rustled in the trees, and the clouds passed very close over his head.

Er trat an die Thür und klopfte an.   3.20

He approached the door and knocked.

Als er zum drittenmal geklopft hatte,   3.21

When he had knocked for the third time,

öffnete eine Alte mit braunem Gesicht und roten Augen die Thür;   3.22

an old woman with a brown face and red eyes opened the door;

sie hatte eine Brille auf ihrer langen Nase und sah ihn scharf an, dann fragte sie, was sein Begehren wäre.   3.23

she had spectacles on her long nose and looked at him sharply, then she asked what he wanted.

3.24 »Einlaß, Kost und Nachtlager.«
"Admission, board and lodging for the night."

3.25 antwortete der Trommler. »Das sollst du haben.«
replied the drummer. "You shall have that."

3.26 sagte die Alte,
said the old woman,

3.27 »wenn du dafür drei Arbeiten, verrichten willst.«
"if you will do three jobs for it."

3.28 »Warum nicht.« antwortete er, »ich scheue keine
Arbeit,
"Why not." he replied, "I don't shy away from any work,

3.29 und wenn sie noch so schwer ist.« Die Alte ließ ihn
ein,
no matter how hard it is." The old woman let him in,

3.30 gab ihm Essen und abends ein gutes Bett.
gave him food and a good bed in the evening.

3.31 Am Morgen, als er ausgeschlafen hatte, nahm die
Alte einen Fingerhut von ihrem dürren Finger,
reichte ihn dem Trommler hin und sagte:
In the morning, when he had slept well, the old woman
took a thimble from her scrawny finger, handed it to the
drummer and said:

3.32 »Jetzt geh an die Arbeit und schöpfe den Teich
draußen mit diesem Fingerhut aus;
"Now go to work and scoop out the pond outside with this
thimble;

aber ehe es Nacht wird, mußt du fertig sein, und alle Fische, die in dem Wasser sind, müssen nach ihrer Art und Größe ausgesucht und nebeneinander gelegt sein.« 3.33

but before night falls, you must be finished, and all the fish in the water must be selected according to their species and size and placed next to each other."

»Das ist eine seltsame Arbeit.« sagte der Trommler, 3.34

"That is strange work." said the drummer,

ging aber zu dem Teich und fing an zu schöpfen. 3.35

but he went to the pond and began to draw.

Er schöpfte den ganzen Morgen, aber was kann man mit einem Fingerhut bei einem großen Wasser ausrichten, und wenn man tausend Jahre schöpft? 3.36

He drew all the morning, but what can one do with a thimble in a large body of water, and if one draws for a thousand years?

Als es Mittag war, dachte er: 3.37

When it was noon, he thought,

»Es ist alles umsonst und ist einerlei, ob ich arbeite oder nicht.« 3.38

"It's all for nothing and it doesn't matter whether I work or not."

hielt ein und setzte sich nieder. 3.39

He stopped and sat down.

Da kam ein Mädchen aus dem Hause gegangen, stellte ihm ein Körbchen mit Essen hin und sprach, 3.40

Then a girl came out of the house, put a basket of food in front of him and said,

3.41 »Du sitzest da so traurig, was fehlt dir?«
"You are sitting there so sad, what are you missing?"

3.42 Er blickte es an und sah, daß es wunderschön war. »Ach.«
He looked at it and saw that it was beautiful. "Ah."

3.43 sagte er, »ich kann die erste Arbeit nicht vollbringen,
said he, "I cannot do the first work,

3.44 wie wird es mit den anderen werden?
how will it be with the others?

3.45 Ich bin ausgegangen, eine Königstochter zu suchen, die hier wohnen soll, aber ich habe sie nicht gefunden;
I went out to look for a king's daughter to live here, but I have not found her;

3.46 ich will weiter gehen.«
I will go on."

3.47 »Bleib hier.« sagte das Mädchen,
"Stay here." said the girl,

3.48 »ich will dir aus deiner Not helfen. Du bist müde,
"I will help you out of your trouble. You are tired,

3.49 lege deinen Kopf in meinen Schoß und schlafe.
lay your head in my lap and sleep.

3.50 Wenn du wieder aufwachst, so ist die Arbeit gethan.«
When you wake up again, the work is done."

3.51 Der Trommler ließ sich das nicht zweimal sagen.
The drummer didn't need to be told twice.

Sobald ihm die Augen zufielen,   3.52
As soon as his eyes closed,

drehte sie einen Wunschring und sprach: »Wasser   3.53
herauf,
she spun a wishing ring and said: "Water up,

Fische heraus.«.   3.54
fish out.".

Alsbald stieg das Wasser wie ein weißer Nebel in die   3.55
Höhe und zog mit den anderen Wolken fort, und die
Fische schnalzten, sprangen ans Ufer und legten sich
nebeneinander, jeder nach seiner Größe und Art!
Immediately the water rose up like a white mist and moved
away with the other clouds, and the fish snapped, jumped
onto the shore and lay down next to each other, each
according to its size and species!

Als der Trommler erwachte, sah er mit Erstaunen,   3.56
daß alles vollbracht war.
When the drummer awoke, he was astonished to see that
everything had been accomplished.

Aber das Mädchen sprach,   3.57
But the girl said,

»Einer von den Fischen liegt nicht bei seinesgleichen,   3.58
"One of the fish is not lying with his own kind,

sondern ganz allein.   3.59
but all alone.

Wenn die Alte heute abend kommt und sieht, daß   3.60
alles geschehen ist, was sie verlangt hat, so wird sie
fragen,
When the old woman comes this evening and sees that all
she has asked for has been done, she will ask,

246

3.61 ›Was soll dieser Fisch allein?‹
'What is this fish for alone?'

3.62 Dann wirf ihr den Fisch ins Angesicht und sprich,
Then throw the fish in her face and say,

3.63 ›Der soll für dich sein, alte Hexe.‹
'It shall be for you, old witch.'

3.64 Abends kam die Alte, und als sie die Frage gethan
hatte, so warf er ihr den Fisch ins Gesicht.
In the evening the old woman came, and when she had
asked the question, he threw the fish in her face.

3.65 Sie stellte sich, als merkte sie es nicht, und schwieg
still, aber sie blickte ihn mit boshaften Augen an.
She pretended not to notice, and was silent, but she looked
at him with malicious eyes.

3.66 Am anderen Morgen sprach sie,
The next morning she said,

3.67 »Gestern hast du es zu leicht gehabt,
"Yesterday you had it too easy,

3.68 ich muß dir schwerere Arbeit geben.
I must give you harder work.

3.69 Heute mußt du den ganzen Wald umhauen, das Holz
in Scheite spalten und in Klaftern legen, und am
Abend muß alles fertig sein.«
Today you must cut down the whole forest, split the wood
into logs and lay them in cribs, and by evening everything
must be ready."

3.70 Sie gab ihm eine Axt, einen Schläger und zwei Keile.
She gave him an axe, a mallet and two wedges.

Aber die Axt war von Blei,   3.71
But the axe was made of lead,

der Schläger und die Keile waren von Blech.   3.72
the mallet and the wedges were made of sheet metal.

Als er anfing zu hauen,   3.73
When he started to chop,

so legte sich die Axt um und Schläger und Keile   3.74
drückten sich zusammen.
the axe folded over and the mallet and wedges pressed
together.

Er wußte sich nicht zu helfen,   3.75
He didn't know what to do,

aber mittags kam das Mädchen wieder mit dem Essen   3.76
und tröstete ihn.
but at midday the girl came back with the food and
comforted him.

»Lege deinen Kopf in meinen Schoß.« sagte sie,   3.77
"Lay your head in my lap." she said,

»und schlafe: wenn du aufwachst, so ist die Arbeit   3.78
gethan.«
"and sleep: when you wake up, the work will be done."

Sie drehte ihren Wunschring, in dem Augenblick   3.79
sank der Wald mit Krachen zusammen, das Holz
spaltete sich von selbst und legte sich in Klaftern
zusammen;
She turned her wishing-ring, and at that moment the forest
sank down with a crash, the wood split by itself, and lay
down in crags;

3.80 **es war, als ob unsichtbare Riesen die Arbeit vollbrächten.**
it was as if invisible giants were doing the work.

3.81 **Als er aufwachte, sagte das Mädchen: »Siehst du,**
When he woke up, the girl said, "You see,

3.82 **das Holz ist geklaftert und gelegt;**
the wood has been felled and laid;

3.83 **nur ein einziger Ast ist übrig, aber wenn die Alte heute abend kommt und fragt, was der Ast solle, so gieb ihr damit einen Schlag und sprich,**
there is only one branch left, but when the old woman comes tonight and asks what the branch is for, give her a blow with it and say,

3.84 **»Der soll für dich sein, du Hexe.« Die Alte kam.**
"It's for you, you witch." The old woman came.

3.85 **»Siehst du.« sprach sie,**
"You see." she said,

3.86 **»wie leicht die Arbeit war; aber für wen liegt der Ast noch da?«**
"how easy the work was, but who else is the branch for?"

3.87 **»Für dich, du Hexe.«**
"For you, you witch."

3.88 **antwortete er und gab ihr einen Schlag damit.**
he answered, and gave her a blow with it.

3.89 **Aber sie that, als fühlte sie es nicht, lachte höhnisch und sprach:**
But she pretended not to feel it, laughed scornfully, and said,

»Morgen früh sollst du alles Holz auf einen Haufen legen, es anzünden und verbrennen.« 3.90

"Tomorrow morning you shall put all the wood in a heap, set fire to it, and burn it."

Er stand mit Anbruch des Tages auf und fing an das Holz herbeizuholen, 3.91

He got up at dawn and began to fetch the wood,

aber wie kann ein einziger Mensch einen ganzen Wald zusammentragen? 3.92

but how could one man gather a whole forest?

Die Arbeit rückte nicht fort. 3.93

The work did not progress.

Doch das Mädchen verließ ihn nicht in der Not: 3.94

But the girl did not leave him in need:

es brachte ihm mittags seine Speise, und als er gegessen hatte, legte er seinen Kopf in den Schoß und schlief ein. 3.95

she brought him his food at noon, and when he had eaten, he put his head in her lap and fell asleep.

Bei seinem Erwachen brannte der ganze Holzstoß in einer ungeheuren Flamme, 3.96

When he awoke,

die ihre Zungen bis in den Himmel ausstreckte. 3.97

the whole pile of wood was ablaze with an immense flame that stretched its tongues to the sky.

»Hör mich an.« sprach das Mädchen, 3.98

"Listen to me." said the girl,

3.99 »wenn die Hexe kommt, wird sie dir allerlei
auftragen:
"when the witch comes, she will tell you all sorts of things:

3.100 thust du ohne Furcht, was sie verlangt, so kann sie
dir nichts anhaben;
if you do what she asks without fear, she can do you no
harm;

3.101 fürchtest du dich aber,
but if you are afraid,

3.102 so packt dich das Feuer und verzehrt dich.
the fire will seize you and consume you.

3.103 Zuletzt, wenn du alles gethan hast, so packe sie mit
beiden Händen und wirf sie mitten in die Glut.«
At last, when thou hast done all, seize her with both hands
and throw her into the midst of the blaze."

3.104 Das Mädchen ging fort, und die Alte kam
herangeschlichen.
The girl went away, and the old woman came creeping up.

3.105 »Hu! mich friert.« sagte sie,
"Hoo! I am cold." she said,

3.106 »aber das ist ein Feuer, das brennt, das wärmt mir die
alten Knochen, da wird mir wohl.
"but this is a fire that burns, it warms my old bones, and I
feel well.

3.107 Aber dort liegt ein Klotz, der will nicht brennen, den
hol mir heraus.
But there's a log lying there that won't burn,
get it out for me.

Hast du das noch gethan, so bist du frei und kannst ziehen, wohin du willst.

3.108

Once you've done that, you're free to go wherever you want.

Nur munter hin ein.«

3.109

Just go on your way."

Der Trommler besann sich nicht lange, sprang mitten in die Flammen, aber sie thaten ihm nichts, nicht einmal die Haare konnten sie ihm versengen.

3.110

The drummer did not think twice and jumped into the flames, but they did him no harm, they could not even scorch his hair.

Er trug den Klotz heraus und legte ihn hin.

3.111

He carried the log out and laid it down.

Kaum aber hatte das Holz die Erde berührt, so verwandelte es sich und das schöne Mädchen stand vor ihm, das ihm in der Not geholfen hatte, und an den seidenen goldglänzenden Kleidern, die es an hatte, merkte er wohl, daß es die Königstochter war.

3.112

But no sooner had the wood touched the ground than it changed, and the beautiful girl who had helped him in his trouble stood before him, and by the silken, shining golden clothes she wore, he knew that she was the king's daughter.

Aber die Alte lachte giftig und sprach:

3.113

But the old woman laughed venomously and said,

»Du meinst, du hättest sie, aber du hast sie noch nicht.«

3.114

"You think you have her, but you haven't got her yet."

3.115 Eben wollte sie auf das Mädchen losgehen und es fortziehen, da packte er die Alte mit beiden Händen, hob sie in die Höhe und warf sie den Flammen in den Rachen, die über ihr zusammenschlugen, als freuten sie sich, daß sie eine Hexe verzehren sollten.

Just as she was about to go at the girl and drag her away, he seized the old woman with both hands, lifted her up and threw her into the jaws of the flames, which burst over her as if they were rejoicing that they were to consume a witch.

4.1 Die Königstochter blickte darauf den Trommler an, und als sie sah, daß es ein schöner Jüngling war, und bedachte, daß er sein Leben daran gesetzt hatte, um sie zu erlösen, so reichte sie ihm die Hand und sprach,

The king's daughter then looked at the drummer, and when she saw that he was a handsome youth, and considered that he had staked his life to redeem her, she held out her hand to him and said,

4.2 »Du hast alles für mich gewagt,

"You have risked everything for me,

4.3 aber ich will auch für dich alles thun.

but I will do everything for you too.

4.4 Versprichst du mir deine Treue,

If you promise to be faithful to me,

4.5 so sollst du mein Gemahl werden.

you shall be my husband.

4.6 An Reichtümern fehlt es uns nicht, wir haben genug an dem, was die Hexe hier zusammengetragen hat.«

We are not lacking in riches, we have enough of what the witch has gathered here."

Sie führte ihn in das Haus, da standen Kisten und Kästen, die mit ihren Schätzen angefüllt waren. 4.7
She led him into the house, where there were chests and boxes filled with her treasures.

Sie ließen Gold und Silber liegen und nahmen nur die Edelsteine. 4.8
They left the gold and silver and only took the precious stones.

Sie wollte nicht länger auf dem Glasberg bleiben, 4.9
She didn't want to stay on the glass mountain any longer,

da sprach er zu ihr: 4.10
so he said to her:

»Setze dich zu mir auf meinen Sattel, so fliegen wir hinab wie Vögel.« 4.11
"Sit with me on my saddle and we'll fly down like birds."

»Der alte Sattel gefällt mir nicht.« sagte sie, 4.12
"I don't like the old saddle." she said,

»ich brauche nur an meinem Wunschring zu drehen, so sind wir zu Haus.« 4.13
"I only need to turn my favorite ring and we'll be home."

»Wohlan.« antwortete der Trommler, 4.14
"Very well." replied the drummer,

»so wünsch uns vor das Stadtthor.« 4.15
"so wish us outside the city gate."

Im Nu waren sie dort, der Trommler aber sprach: 4.16
In a moment they were there, but the drummer said,

4.17 »Ich will erst zu meinen Eltern gehen und ihnen Nachricht geben, harre mein hier auf dem Feld, ich will bald zurück sein.«

"I will first go to my parents and give them news, wait for me here in the field, I will soon be back."

4.18 »Ach.« sagte die Königstochter,

"Oh." said the king's daughter,

4.19 »ich bitte dich, nimm dich in acht, küsse deine Eltern bei deiner Ankunft nicht auf die rechte Wange, denn sonst wirst du alles vergessen, und ich bleibe hier allein und verlassen auf dem Feld zurück.«

"I beg you to be careful, don't kiss your parents on the right cheek when you arrive, otherwise you will forget everything, and I will be left here alone and abandoned in the field."

4.20 »Wie kann ich dich vergessen?«

"How can I forget you?"

4.21 sagte er und versprach ihr in die rechte Hand, recht bald wieder zu kommen.

he said and promised her in his right hand that he would come back soon.

4.22 Als er in sein väterliches Haus trat, wußte niemand, wer er war, so hatte er sich verändert, denn die drei Tage, die er auf dem Glasberg zugebracht hatte, waren drei lange Jahre gewesen.

When he entered his father's house, no one knew who he was, he had changed so much, for the three days he had spent on the glass mountain had been three long years.

Da gab er sich zu erkennen, und seine Eltern fielen   4.23
ihm vor Freude um den Hals, und er war so bewegt
in seinem Herzen, daß er sie auf beide Wangen küßte
und an die Worte des Mädchens nicht dachte.

Then he made himself known, and his parents flung their
arms round his neck for joy, and he was so moved in his
heart that he kissed them on both cheeks, and thought
nothing of the girl's words.

Wie er ihnen aber den Kuß auf die rechte Wange   4.24
gegeben hatte,

But as soon as he had kissed them on the right cheek,

verschwand ihm jeder Gedanke an die Königstochter.   4.25

all thought of the King's daughter vanished from his mind.

Er leerte seine Taschen aus und legte Hände voll der   4.26
größten Edelsteine auf den Tisch.

He emptied his pockets and laid hands full of the largest
precious stones on the table.

Die Eltern wußten gar nicht, was sie mit dem   4.27
Reichtum anfangen sollten.

The parents did not know what to do with the wealth.

Da baute der Vater ein prächtiges Schloß, von Gärten,   4.28
Wäldern und Wiesen umgeben, als wenn ein Fürst
darin wohnen sollte.

So the father built a magnificent castle, surrounded
by gardens, woods and meadows, as if a prince were to
live in it.

Und als es fertig war, sagte die Mutter: 4.29

And when it was finished, the mother said:

»Ich habe ein Mädchen für dich ausgesucht,   4.30

"I have chosen a girl for you,

4.31 in drei Tagen soll die Hochzeit sein.«
the wedding will take place in three days."

4.32 Der Sohn war mit allem zufrieden, was die Eltern
wollten.
The son was happy with everything his parents wanted.

5.1 Die arme Königstochter hatte lange vor der Stadt
gestanden und auf die Rückkehr des Jünglings
gewartet.
The poor king's daughter had been standing outside the
town for a long time waiting for the young man to return.

5.2 Als es Abend ward, sprach sie:
When evening came, she said,

5.3 »Gewiß hat er seine Eltern auf die rechte Wange
geküßt und hat mich vergessen.«
"Surely he has kissed his parents on the right cheek and
forgotten me."

5.4 Ihr Herz war voll Trauer,
Her heart was full of sorrow,

5.5 sie wünschte sich in ein einsames Waldhäuschen und
wollte nicht wieder an den Hof ihres Vaters zurück.
she wished herself away in a lonely cottage in the woods
and did not want to return to her father's court.

5.6 Jeden Abend ging sie in die Stadt und ging an des
Trommlers Haus vorüber:
Every evening she went into the town and passed the
drummer's house:

5.7 er sah sie manchmal, aber er kannte sie nicht mehr.
he saw her sometimes, but he no longer knew her.

Endlich hörte sie die Leute sagen: 5.8
At last she heard people saying,

»Morgen wird seine Hochzeit gefeiert.« Da sprach sie,   5.9
"Tomorrow his wedding will be celebrated." Then she said,

»Ich will versuchen, ob ich sein Herz wieder   5.10
gewinne.«
"I will see if I can win his heart again."

Als der erste Hochzeitstag gefeiert ward,   5.11
When the first wedding day was celebrated,

da drehte sie ihren Wunschring und sprach: 5.12
she turned her wish ring and said:

»Ein Kleid so glänzend wie die Sonne.«   5.13
"A dress as brilliant as the sun."

Alsbald lag das Kleid vor ihr und war so glänzend, als   5.14
wenn es aus lauter Sonnenstrahlen gewebt wäre.
Immediately the dress lay before her and was as brilliant as
if it had been woven from the sun's rays.

Als alle Gäste sich versammelt hatten, so trat sie in   5.15
den Saal.
When all the guests had gathered, she entered the hall.

Jedermann wunderte sich über das schöne Kleid, am   5.16
meisten die Braut, und da schöne Kleider ihre größte
Lust waren, so ging sie zu der Fremden und fragte, ob
sie es ihr verkaufen wollte.
Everyone was astonished at the beautiful dress, especially
the bride, and as beautiful dresses were her greatest delight,
she went to the stranger and asked if she would sell it to
her.

5.17 »Für Geld nicht.« antwortete sie,

"Not for money." she replied,

5.18 »aber wenn ich die erste Nacht vor der Thür verweilen darf, wo der Bräutigam schläft, so will ich es hingeben.«

"but if I may stay the first night at the door where the bridegroom sleeps, I will give it away."

5.19 Die Braut konnte ihr Verlangen nicht bezwingen und willigte ein, aber sie mischte dem Bräutigam einen Schlaftrunk in seinen Nachtwein, wovon er in tiefen Schlaf verfiel.

The bride could not restrain her desire and consented, but she mixed a nightcap into the bridegroom's night wine, from which he fell into a deep sleep.

5.20 Als nun alles still geworden war, so kauerte sich die Königstochter vor die Thür der Schlafkammer, öffnete sie ein wenig und rief hinein:

When all was quiet, the king's daughter crouched down at the door of the bedchamber, opened it a little and called in:

»Trommler, Trommler, hör mich an,

"Drummer, drummer, listen to me,

hast du mich denn ganz vergessen?

Have you forgotten all about me?

hast du auf dem Glasberg nicht bei mir gesessen?

Didn't you sit with me on the glass mountain?

habe ich vor der Hexe nicht bewahrt dein Leben?

did I not save your life from the witch?

hast du mir auf Treue nicht
die Hand gegeben?

did you not shake my
hand in fidelity?

Trommler, Trommler, hör
mich an.«

Drummer, drummer,
listen to me."

Aber es war alles vergeblich, der Trommler wachte
nicht auf, und als der Morgen anbrach, mußte
die Königstochter unverrichteter Dinge wieder
fortgehen.

7.1

But it was all in vain, the drummer did not wake up, and
when morning came, the king's daughter had to leave
without having achieved anything.

Am zweiten Abend drehte sie ihren Wunschring und
sprach,

7.2

On the second evening she turned her wishing-ring and
said,

»Ein Kleid so silbern als der Mond.«

7.3

"A dress as silver as the moon."

Als sie mit dem Kleid, das so zart war wie der
Mondschein, bei dem Fest erschien, erregte sie
wieder das Verlangen der Braut und gab es ihr für
die Erlaubnis, auch die zweite Nacht vor der Tür der
Schlafkammer zubringen zu dürfen.

7.4

When she appeared at the feast with the dress, which was
as delicate as the moonlight, she again aroused the bride's
desire and gave it to her for permission to spend the second
night at the door of the bedchamber.

Da rief sie in nächtlicher Stille:

7.5

Then she cried out in the silence of the night:

»Trommler, Trommler, hör mich an,	"Drummer, drummer, listen to me,
hast du mich denn ganz vergessen?	Have you forgotten all about me?
hast du auf dem Glasberg nicht bei mir gesessen?	Didn't you sit with me on the glass mountain?
habe ich vor der Hexe nicht bewahrt dein Leben?	did I not save your life from the witch?
hast du mir auf Treue nicht die Hand gegeben?	did you not shake my hand in fidelity?
Trommler, Trommler, hör mich an.«	Drummer, drummer, listen to me."

9.1 Aber der Trommler, von dem Schlaftrunk betäubt, war nicht zu erwecken.
But the drummer, stunned by the sleeping potion, could not be awakened.

9.2 Traurig ging sie den Morgen wieder zurück in ihr Waldhaus.
Sadly, she went back to her forest house in the morning.

9.3 Aber die Leute im Hause hatten die Klage des fremden Mädchens gehört und erzählten dem Bräutigam davon;
But the people in the house had heard the strange girl's complaint and told the bridegroom about it;

sie sagten ihm auch, daß es ihm nicht möglich   9.4
gewesen wäre, etwas davon zu vernehmen, weil
sie ihm einen Schlaftrunk in den Wein geschüttet
hätten.

they also told him that he had not been able to hear any of it
because they had poured a sleeping draught into his wine.

Am dritten Abend drehte die Königstochter den   9.5
Wunschring und sprach,

On the third evening the king's daughter turned the
wishing-ring, and said,

»Ein Kleid flimmernd wie Sterne.«   9.6

"A dress shimmering like stars."

Als sie sich darin auf dem Fest zeigte, war die Braut   9.7
über die Pracht des Kleides, das die anderen weit
übertraf, ganz außer sich und sprach,

When she showed herself in it at the feast, the bride was
beside herself at the splendor of the dress, which far
surpassed the others, and said,

»Ich soll und muß es haben.«   9.8

"I shall and must have it."

Das Mädchen gab es, wie die anderen, für die   9.9
Erlaubnis, die Nacht vor der Thür des Bräutigams
zuzubringen.

The girl gave it, like the others, for permission to spend the
night at the bridegroom's door.

Der Bräutigam aber trank den Wein nicht, der ihm   9.10
vor dem Schlafengehen gereicht wurde, sondern goß
ihn hinter das Bett.

The bridegroom, however, did not drink the wine which
was given him before going to bed, but poured it behind the
bed.

9.11 Und als alles im Hause still geworden war, so hörte er eine sanfte Stimme, die ihn anrief:

And when all was quiet in the house, he heard a gentle voice calling to him:

»Trommler, Trommler, hör mich an,	"Drummer, drummer, listen to me,
hast du mich denn ganz vergessen?	Have you forgotten all about me?
hast du auf dem Glasberg nicht bei mir gesessen?	Didn't you sit with me on the glass mountain?
habe ich vor der Hexe nicht bewahrt dein Leben?	did I not save your life from the witch?
hast du mir auf Treue nicht die Hand gegeben?	did you not shake my hand in fidelity?
Trommler, Trommler, hör mich an.«	Drummer, drummer, listen to me."

11.1 Plötzlich kam ihm das Gedächtnis wieder. »Ach.« rief er,

Suddenly his memory came back to him. "Alas." he cried,

11.2 »wie habe ich so treulos handeln können, aber der Kuß, den ich meinen Eltern in der Freude meines Herzens auf die rechte Wange gegeben habe, der ist schuld daran, der hat mich betäubt.«

"how could I have acted so unfaithfully, but the kiss I gave my parents on the right cheek in the joy of my heart is to blame, it stunned me."

11.3 Er sprang auf,

He jumped up,

nahm die Königstochter bei der Hand und führte sie zu dem Bett seiner Eltern.

11.4

took the king's daughter by the hand and led her to his parents' bed.

»Das ist meine rechte Braut.« sprach er,

11.5

"This is my right bride." he said,

»wenn ich die andere heirate, so thue ich großes Unrecht.«

11.6

"if I marry the other, I shall do great wrong."

Die Eltern, als sie hörten, wie alles sich zugetragen hatte, willigten ein.

11.7

The parents, when they heard how everything had happened, consented.

Da wurden die Lichter im Saal wieder angezündet, Pauken und Trompeten herbeigeholt, die Freunde und Verwandten eingeladen, wiederzukommen, und die wahre Hochzeit ward mit großer Freude gefeiert.

11.8

Then the lights in the hall were lit again, drums and trumpets were brought in, friends and relatives were invited to come back, and the real wedding was celebrated with great joy.

Die erste Braut behielt die schönen Kleider zur Entschädigung und gab sich zufrieden.

11.9

The first bride kept the beautiful dresses as compensation and was satisfied.

Die Kornähre

The Ear of Corn

^{1.1} **Vorzeiten, als Gott noch selbst auf Erden wandelte, da war die Fruchtbarkeit des Bodens viel größer als sie jetzt ist:**

In ancient times, when God himself still walked the earth, the fertility of the soil was much greater than it is now:

^{1.2} **damals trugen die Ähren nicht fünfzig - oder sechzigfältig,**

in those days the ears of corn were not fifty or sixty-fold,

^{1.3} **sondern vier - bis fünfhundertfältig.**

but four to five hundred-fold.

^{1.4} **Da wuchsen die Körner am Halm von unten bis oben hinauf;**

The grains grew on the stalk from the bottom to the top;

^{1.5} **so lang er war, so lang war auch die Ähre.**

the longer it was, the longer the ear was.

Aber wie die Menschen sind, im Überfluß achten sie 1.6
des Segens nicht mehr, der von Gott kommt, werden
gleichgiltig und leichtsinnig.

But as people are, in their abundance they no longer pay
attention to the blessing that comes from God and become
indifferent and careless.

Eines Tages ging eine Frau an einem Kornfeld vorbei, 1.7
und ihr kleines Kind, das neben ihr sprang, fiel in
eine Pfütze und beschmutzte sein Kleidchen.

One day a woman was walking past a cornfield and her little
child, who was jumping beside her, fell into a puddle and
soiled his little dress.

Da riß die Mutter eine Handvoll der schönen Ähren 1.8
ab und reinigte ihm damit das Kleid.

So the mother tore off a handful of the beautiful ears of
corn and used them to clean his dress.

Als der Herr, der eben vorüberkam, das sah, zürnte er 1.9
und sprach,

When the Lord, who was just passing by, saw this, he was
angry and said,

»Fortan soll der Kornhalm keine Ähre mehr tragen; 1.10

"From now on, the corn stalk shall no longer bear an ear of
corn;

die Menschen sind der himmlischen Gabe nicht 1.11
länger wert.«

people are no longer worthy of the heavenly gift."

1.12 Die Umstehenden, die das hörten, erschraken, fielen auf die Knie und flehten, daß er noch etwas möchte an dem Halm stehen lassen; wenn sie selbst es auch nicht verdienten, doch der unschuldigen Hühner wegen, die sonst verhungern müßten.

The bystanders who heard this were frightened, fell on their knees and begged him to leave something on the stalk, even if they themselves did not deserve it, but for the sake of the innocent chickens, which would otherwise have to starve.

1.13 Der Herr, der ihr Elend voraussah, erbarmte sich und gewährte die Bitte.

The Lord, who foresaw their misery, took pity on them and granted their request.

1.14 Also blieb noch oben die Ähre übrig,

So the ear of corn remained at the top,

1.15 wie sie jetzt wächst.

just as it is growing now.

Der Grabhügel

The Burial Mound

1.1 **Ein reicher Bauer stand eines Tages in seinem Hofe und schaute nach seinen Feldern und Gärten:**
A rich farmer stood one day in his yard and looked at his fields and gardens:

1.2 **das Korn wuchs kräftig heran und die Obstbäume hingen voll Früchte.**
the grain was growing vigorously and the fruit trees were full of fruit.

1.3 **Das Getreide des vorigen Jahres lag noch in so mächtigen Haufen auf dem Boden, daß es kaum die Balken tragen konnten.**
Last year's grain was still lying on the ground in such huge heaps that the beams could hardly bear it.

1.4 **Dann ging er in den Stall, da standen die gemästeten Ochsen, die fetten Kühe und die spiegelglatten Pferde.**
Then he went into the stable, where the fattened oxen, the fat cows and the sleek horses stood.

Endlich ging er in seine Stube zurück und warf seine
Blicke auf die eisernen Kästen, 1.5
At last he went back into his parlor,

in welchen sein Geld lag. 1.6
and cast his eyes on the iron boxes in which his money lay.

Als er so stand und seinen Reichtum übersah, 1.7
As he stood there looking at his wealth,

klopfte es auf einmal heftig bei ihm an. 1.8
suddenly there was a heavy knock on his door.

Es klopfte aber nicht an die Thür seiner Stube, 1.9
It did not knock at the door of his parlor,

sondern an die Thür seines Herzens. 1.10
but at the door of his heart.

Sie that sich auf Und er hörte eine Stimme, die zu
ihm sprach: 1.11
It opened and he heard a voice saying to him:

»Hast du den Deinigen damit wohlgethan? 1.12
"Have you done good to your own?

Hast du die Not der Armen angesehen? 1.13
Have you seen the need of the poor?

Hast du mit den Hungrigen dein Brot geteilt? 1.14
Did you share your bread with the hungry?

War dir genug, 1.15
Was what you had enough,

1.16 was du besaßest oder hast du noch immer mehr
verlangt?«
or did you still ask for more?"

1.17 Das Herz zögerte nicht mit der Antwort:
The heart did not hesitate to answer:

1.18 »Ich bin hart und unerbittlich gewesen und habe den
Meinigen niemals etwas Gutes erzeigt.
"I have been hard and unrelenting and have never done
anything good for my own.

1.19 Ist ein Armer gekommen, so habe ich mein Auge
weggewendet.
If a poor person came, I turned my eye away.

1.20 Ich habe mich um Gott nicht bekümmert,
I have not cared for God,

1.21 sondern nur an die Mehrung meines Reichtums
gedacht.
but have only thought of increasing my wealth.

1.22 Wäre alles mein eigen gewesen, was der Himmel
bedeckte, dennoch hätte ich nicht genug gehabt.«
If all that the sky covered had been mine, I would still not
have had enough."

1.23 Als er diese Antwort vernahm, erschrak er heftig;
When he heard this answer, he was violently frightened;

1.24 die Knie fingen an ihm zu zittern und er mußte sich
niedersetzen.
his knees began to tremble and he had to sit down.

1.25 Da klopfte es abermals an,
Then there came another knock,

aber es klopfte an die Thür seiner Stube.   1.26
but it was at the door of his parlor.

Es war sein Nachbar, ein armer Mann, der ein   1.27
Häufchen Kinder hatte, die er nicht mehr sättigen
konnte.
It was his neighbor, a poor man who had a heap of children
he could no longer feed.

»Ich weiß.« dachte der Arme, »mein Nachbar ist   1.28
reich,
"I know." thought the poor man, "my neighbor is rich,

aber er ist ebenso hart;   1.29
but he is just as hard;

ich glaube nicht, daß er mir hilft, aber meine Kinder   1.30
schreien nach Brot, da will ich es wagen.«
I don't think he will help me, but my children are crying for
bread, so I will dare."

Er sprach zu dem Reichen:,   1.31
He said to the rich man,

»Ihr gebt nicht leicht etwas von dem Eurigen weg,   1.32
aber ich stehe da wie einer, dem das Wasser bis an
den Kopf geht:
"You do not easily give away any of your own, but I stand
there like one who has water up to his head:

meine Kinder hungern, leiht mir vier Malter Körn.«   1.33
my children are hungry, lend me four malt of grain."

– Der Reiche sah ihn lange an;   1.34
– The rich man looked at him for a long time;

1.35 da begann der erste Sonnenstrahl der Milde einen Tropfen von dem Eis der Habsucht abzuschmelzen.

then the first ray of mildness began to melt a drop from the ice of greed.

1.36 »Vier Malter will ich dir nicht leihen.« antwortete er,

"I will not lend you four maltings." he answered,

1.37 »sondern acht will ich dir schenken,

"but I will give you eight,

1.38 aber eine Bedingung mußt du erfüllen.«

but you must fulfill one condition."

1.39 »Was soll ich thun?« sprach der Arme. »Wenn ich tot bin,

"What shall I do?" said the poor man. "When I am dead,

1.40 sollst du drei Nächte an meinem Grabe wachen.«

you shall watch over my grave for three nights."

1.41 Dem Bauer ward bei dem Antrag unheimlich zu Mute; doch in der Not, in der er sich befand, hätte er alles bewilligt: er sagte also zu und trug das Korn heim.

The farmer felt uneasy at the proposal, but in the trouble he was in he would have granted anything, so he agreed and carried the corn home.

2.1 Es war, als hätte der Reiche vorausgesehen, was geschehen würde, nach drei Tagen fiel er plötzlich tot zur Erde; man mußte nicht recht, wie es zugegangen war, aber niemand trauerte um ihn.

It was as if the rich man had foreseen what would happen; after three days he suddenly fell to the ground dead; it was not clear how it had happened, but no one mourned him.

Als er bestattet war, fiel dem Armen sein Versprechen
ein: gern wäre er davon entbunden gewesen, aber er
dachte:

2.2

When he was buried, the poor man remembered his
promise: he would gladly have been released from it, but he
thought,

»Er hat sich gegen dich doch mildthätig erwiesen,
du hast mit seinem Korn deine hungrigen Kinder
gesättigt, und wäre das auch nicht, du hast einmal
das Versprechen gegeben und mußt es halten.«

2.3

"He has shown himself charitable to you, you have fed your
hungry children with his grain, and even if you had not,
you once made the promise and must keep it."

Bei einbrechender Nacht ging er auf den Friedhof
und setzte sich auf den Grabhügel.

2.4

As night fell, he went to the cemetery and sat down on the
burial mound.

Es war alles still,

2.5

All was quiet,

nur der Mond schien über die Grabhügel und
manchmal flog eine Eule vorbei und ließ ihre
kläglichen Töne hören.

2.6

only the moon shone over the grave mounds and
sometimes an owl flew by and made its mournful sounds.

Als die Sonne aufging,

2.7

When the sun rose,

begab sich der Arme ungefährdet heim und ebenso
ging die zweite Nacht ruhig vorüber.

2.8

the poor man went home safely and the second night also
passed quietly.

274

2.9 Den Abend des dritten Tages empfand er eine besondere Angst, es war ihm, als stände noch etwas bevor.

On the evening of the third day, he felt a particular fear, as if something was still to come.

2.10 Als er hinauskam, erblickte er an der Mauer des Kirchhofes einen Mann, den er noch nie gesehen hatte.

When he came out, he saw a man he had never seen before standing by the wall of the churchyard.

2.11 Er war nicht mehr jung,

He was no longer young,

2.12 hatte Narben im Gesicht und seine Augen blickten scharf und feurig umher.

had scars on his face and his eyes were sharp and fiery.

2.13 Er war ganz von einem alten Mantel bedeckt und nur große Reiterstiefeln waren sichtbar.

He was completely covered by an old cloak and only large riding boots were visible.

2.14 »Was sucht Ihr hier?« redete ihn der Bauer an,

"What are you looking for here?" the farmer addressed him,

2.15 »gruselt Euch nicht auf dem einsamen Kirchhof?«

"aren't you creeped out in the lonely churchyard?"

2.16 »Ich suche nichts.« antwortete er,

"I'm not looking for anything." he replied,

2.17 »aber ich fürchte auch nichts.

"but I'm not afraid of anything either.

Ich bin wie der Junge, der ausging, das Gruseln   2.18
zu lernen und sich vergeblich bemühte, der aber
bekam die Königstochter zur Frau und mit ihr große
Reichtümer, und ich bin immer arm geblieben.

I am like the boy who went out to learn to creep and tried in
vain, but he got the king's daughter as his wife and with her
great riches, and I have always remained poor.

Ich bin nichts als ein abgedankter Soldat und will   2.19
hier die Nacht zubringen, weil ich sonst kein Obdach
habe.«

I am nothing but a resigned soldier and want to spend the
night here because I have no other shelter."

»Wenn Ihr keine Furcht habt.« sprach der Bauer,   2.20

"If you have no fear." said the farmer,

»so bleibt bei mir und helft mir dort den Grabhügel   2.21
bewachen.«

"stay with me and help me guard the burial mound."

»Wacht halten ist Sache des Soldaten.« antwortete er,   2.22

"Keeping watch is the soldier's business." he replied,

»was uns hier begegnet, Gutes oder Böses, das wollen   2.23
wir gemeinschaftlich tragen.«

"whatever we encounter here, good or bad, we will bear
together."

Der Bauer schlug ein und sie setzten sich zusammen   2.24
auf das Grab.

The farmer joined in and they sat down together on the
grave.

3.1 Alles blieb still bis Mitternacht, da ertönte auf einmal ein schneidendes Pfeifen in der Luft und die beiden Wächter erblickten den Bösen, der leibhaftig vor ihnen stand.

Everything remained silent until midnight, when suddenly a piercing whistle sounded in the air and the two guards caught sight of the evil one standing before them in the flesh.

3.2 »Fort, ihr Halunken.« rief er ihnen zu,

"Away, you scoundrels." he called to them,

3.3 »der in dem Grabe liegt, ist mein:

"he who lies in the grave is mine:

3.4 ich will ihn holen, und wo ihr nicht weggeht, dreh ich euch die Hälse um.«

I will fetch him, and if you do not leave, I will wring your necks."

3.5 »Herr mit der roten Feder.« sprach der Soldat,

"Sir with the red feather." said the soldier,

3.6 »Ihr seid mein Hauptmann nicht,

"you are not my captain,

3.7 ich brauche Euch nicht zu gehorchen und das Fürchten habe ich noch nicht gelernt.

I do not need to obey you and I have not yet learned to fear you.

3.8 Geht Eurer Wege, wir bleiben hier sitzen.« Der Teufel dachte:

Go your way, we'll sit here." The devil thought:

3.9 »Mit Gold fängst du die zwei Haderlumpen am besten.«

"The best way to catch the two ragamuffins is with gold."

zog gelindere Saiten auf und fragte ganz zutraulich, 3.10
ob sie nicht einen Beutel mit Gold annehmen und
damit heimgehen wollten.
The devil took a softer tone and asked them very trustingly
if they would accept a bag of gold and go home with it.

»Das läßt sich hören.« antwortete der Soldat, 3.11
"That is all very well." replied the soldier,

»aber mit einem Beutel voll Gold ist uns nicht 3.12
gedient;
"but a bag of gold is no use to us;

wenn Ihr so viel Gold geben wollt, als da in einen von 3.13
meinen Stiefeln geht, so wollen wir Euch das Feld
räumen und abziehen.«
if you will give as much gold as will go into one of my boots,
we will clear the field for you and leave."

»So viel habe ich nicht bei mir.« sagte der Teufel, 3.14
"I have not so much with me." said the devil,

»aber ich will es holen: 3.15
"but I will fetch it:

in der benachbarten Stadt wohnt ein Wechsler, der 3.16
mein guter Freund ist, der streckt mir gern so viel
vor.«
there is a money-changer in the neighboring town who is
my good friend, and he will gladly give me so much."

Als der Teufel verschwunden war, zog der Soldat 3.17
seinen linken Stiefel aus und sprach,
When the devil had disappeared, the soldier took off his left
boot and said,

3.18 »Dem Kohlenbrenner wollen wir schon eine Nase drehen:

"We'll give the coal-burner a nose:

3.19 gebt mir nur Euer Messer, Gevatter.«

just give me your knife, father."

3.20 Er schnitt von dem Stiefel die Sohle ab und stellte ihn neben den Hügel in das hohe Gras an den Rand einer halb überwachsenen Grube.

He cut off the sole of the boot and placed it next to the hill in the tall grass on the edge of a half-covered pit.

3.21 »So ist alles gut.« sprach er,

"That's all right." he said,

3.22 »nun kann der Schornsteinfeger kommen.«

"now the chimney sweep can come."

4.1 Beide setzten sich und warteten, es dauerte nicht lange, so kam der Teufel und hatte ein Säckchen Gold in der Hand:

They both sat down and waited, and it wasn't long before the devil arrived with a small bag of gold in his hand:

4.2 »Schüttet es nur hinein.«

"Just pour it in."

4.3 sprach der Soldat und hob den Stiefel ein wenig in die Höhe,

said the soldier, lifting his boot up a little,

4.4 »das wird aber nicht genug sein.«

"but that won't be enough."

4.5 Der Schwarze leerte das Säckchen,

The black man emptied the bag,

das Gold fiel durch und der Stiefel blieb leer.   4.6
the gold fell through and the boot remained empty.

»Dummer Teufel.« rief der Soldat, »es schickt nicht;   4.7
"Stupid devil." cried the soldier, "it's no good;

habe ich es nicht gleich gesagt?   4.8
didn't I tell you at once?

Kehrt nur wieder um und holt mehr.«   4.9
Just turn back and get more."

Der Teufel schüttelte den Kopf,   4.10
The devil shook his head,

ging und kam nach einer Stunde mit einem viel   4.11
größeren Sack unter dem Arm.
left and came back an hour later with a much larger sack
under his arm.

»Nur eingefüllt.« rief der Soldat,   4.12
"Just filled it." cried the soldier,

»aber ich zweifle, daß der Stiefel voll wird.«   4.13
"but I doubt if the boot will be full."

Das Gold klingelte, als es hinabfiel, und der Stiefel   4.14
blieb leer.
The gold rang as it fell, and the boot remained empty.

Der Teufel blickte mit seinen glühenden Augen selbst   4.15
hinein und überzeugte sich von der Wahrheit.
The devil looked into it himself with his glowing eyes and
convinced himself of the truth.

»Ihr habt unverschämt starke Waden.«   4.16
"You have outrageously strong calves."

4.17 rief er und verzog den Mund. »Meint Ihr.«

he exclaimed, his mouth agape. "Do you think."

4.18 erwiderte der Soldat, »ich hätte einen Pferdefuß wie Ihr?

the soldier replied, "that I have a horse's foot like you?

4.19 Seit wann seid Ihr so knauserig?

Since when have you been so stingy?

4.20 Macht, daß Ihr mehr Gold herbeischafft, sonst wird aus unserem Handel nichts.«

You'd better get some more gold, or our bargain will come to nothing."

4.21 Der Unhold trollte sich abermals fort.

The ogre trudged off again.

4.22 Diesmal blieb er länger aus, und als er endlich erschien, keuchte er unter der Last eines Sackes, der auf seiner Schulter lag.

This time he stayed out longer, and when he finally appeared, he was panting under the weight of a sack on his shoulder.

4.23 Er schüttete ihn in den Stiefel, der sich aber so wenig füllte, als vorher.

He poured it into the boot, but it filled as little as before.

4.24 Er ward wütend und wollte dem Soldaten den Stiefel aus der Hand reißen,

He was furious and wanted to snatch the boot out of the soldier's hand,

aber in dem Augenblick drang der erste Strahl der 4.25
aufgehenden Sonne am Himmel herauf und der böse
Geist entfloh mit lautem Geschrei.
but at that moment the first ray of the rising sun appeared
in the sky and the evil spirit fled with a loud scream.

Die arme Seele war gerettet. 4.26
The poor soul was saved.

Der Bauer wollte das Gold teilen, aber der Soldat 5.1
sprach:
The farmer wanted to share the gold, but the soldier said:

»Gieb den Armen was mir zufällt; 5.2
"Give to the poor what is mine;

ich ziehe zu dir in deine Hütte und wir wollen mit 5.3
dem übrigen in Ruhe und Frieden zusammen leben,
solange es Gott gefällt.«
I will join you in your hut and we will live together with the
rest in peace and quiet as long as it pleases God."

Oll Rinkrank

1.1 Dar war mal 'n König wän, un de har 'n Dochter hat, un de har 'n glasen Barg maken laten un har segt, de dar över lopen kun, an to vallen, de schull sin Dochter to 'n Fro hebben.

There was once a king who had a daughter, and he had had a glass bar made and had said that he wanted to have his daughter as his wife.

1.2 Do is dar ok en, de mag de Königsdochter so gärn liden, de vragt den König, of he sin Dochter nich hebben schal?

Then there is one who likes the king's daughter so much that she asks the king if he doesn't want to have her daughter?

1.3 »Ja.« segt de König,

"Yes." says the king,

1.4 »wenn he dar över den Barg lopen kan, an dat he valt, den schal he är hebben.«

"if he can get over the bar to where he is, he should have it."

Do segt de Königsdochter, den wil se dar mit hüm över lopen un wil hüm hollen, wen he war vallen schul. 1.5

Then the king's daughter says that she wants to take him over the bar and wants to fetch him if he was to fall.

Do lopt se dar mit 1.6

Then she loped over with

'nanner över, un as se dar miden up sunt, do glit de Königsdochter ut un valt, un de Glasbarg de deit sick apen un se schütt darin hendal: 1.7

'nanner', and as they were sitting there, the king's daughter slipped out and fell, and the glass bar opened and she poured into it:

un de Brögam de kan nich sen, war se hervorkamen is, den de Barg het sick glick wär to dan. 1.8

and the bridegroom couldn't tell how she had come out, because the bar had fallen down.

Do jammert un went he so väl, un de König is ok so trorig un let den Barg dar wedder weg bräken un ment, he wil är wedder ut krigen, man se könt de Stä ni finnen, wär se hendal vallen is. 1.9

He moaned and cried so much, and the king was so sad that he let the bar break away again and said that he wanted to get it out again, but he couldn't find the bar where it had fallen.

Ünnertüsken is de Königsdochter ganz dep in de Grunt in 'n grote Höl kamen. 1.10

In the meantime, the king's daughter has come to a large wood in the green.

1.11 Do kumt är dar 'n ollen Karl mit 'n ganzen langen grauen Bart to möt un de segt, wen se sin Magd wäsen wil un all don, wat he bevelt, den schal se läven bliven, anners will he är ümbringen.

Then he comes to old Karl with a long gray beard and says that if she wants to wash his maid and do whatever he wants, she should leave him alone, otherwise he will take her away.

1.12 Do deit se all, wat he är segt.

Then she does everything he says.

1.13 'S Morgens den kricht he sin Ledder ut de Task un legt de an den Barg un sticht darmit to 'n Barg henut;

In the morning, he takes his leather out of the task and puts it on the bar and stabs it into the bar;

1.14 un den lukt he de Ledder na sick ümhoch mit sick henup.

and then he pulls the leather up with him.

1.15 Un den mut se sin Äten kaken un sin Bedd maken un all sin Arbeit don, un den, wen he wedder in Hus kumt, den bringt he alltit 'n Hüpen Golt un Sülver mit.

And to him he must make his eyes and his bed and do all his work, and when he comes back home, he always brings him a pile of gold and sweetener.

1.16 As se al väl jaren bi ein wäsen is un al ganz olt wurden is, do het he är Fro Mansrot, un se möt hüm oll Rinkrank heten.

When she had been washing for many years and had become very old, she had her first man's red, and she wanted to have a nice drink.

Do is he ok ins enmal ut, do makt se hüm sin Bedd 1.17
un waskt sin Schöttels, un do makt se de Dören un
Vensters all dicht to, un do is dar so 'n Schuf wäsen,
war 't Lecht herin schint het, dat let se apen.

Then he went inside, she made his bed and washed his
shoes, and then she closed all the doors and windows, and
then she washed such a mess that she let it go.

As d' oll Rinkrank do wedder kumt, 1.18

When the old rinkrank came back,

do klopt he an sin Dör un röpt: »Fro Mansrot, 1.19

he knocked on his door and shouted: "Fro Mansrot,

do mi d' Dör apen.« 1.20

open my door."

»Na.« 1.21

"Well."

segt se, »ik do di, oll Rinkrank, d' Dör nich apen.« 1.22

she says, "I'm not going to open the village for you, old
Rinkrank."

Do segt he: 1.23

Then he says:

»Hir sta ik arme Rinkrank "Hir sta ik arme
            Rinkrank

up min söventeim Benen up min söventeim Benen
lank,   lank,

up min en vergüllen Vot, up min en vergüllen Vot,

Fro Mansrot, wask mi d' Fro Mansrot, wask mi d'
Schöttels.«   Schöttels."

3.1 »'k heb diu Schottels al wusken.« segt se. Do segt he wedder:

"'k heb diu Schottels al wusken." she says. Then he says again:

»Hir sta ik arme Rinkrank	"Hir sta ik arme Rinkrank
Up min söventein Benen lank,	Up min söventein Benen lank,
Up min en vergüllen Vot,	Up min en vergüllen Vot,
Fro Mansrot, mak mi 't Bedd.«	Fro Mansrot, mak mi 't Bedd."

5.1 »'k heb bin Bedd all makt.« segt se. Do segt he wedder:

"'k heb bin Bedd all makt." she says. Then he says again:

»Hir sta ik arme Rinkrank	"Hir sta ik arme Rinkrank
Up min söventein Benen lank,	Up min söventein Benen lank,
Up min en vergüllen Vot,	Up min en vergüllen Vot,
Fro Mansrot, do mi d' Dör apen.«	Fro Mansrot, do mi d' Dör apen."

7.1 Do löpt he all runt üm sin Hus to un süt, dat de lütke Luk dar apen is, do denkt he:

Then he looks around his house and sees that the little hatch is open, so he thinks:

»Du schast doch ins tosen, wat se dar wol makt, warum dat se mi d' Dör wol nich apen don wil.«

"You're wondering what she's doing there, why she won't let me open the door."

7.2

Do wil he dar dör kiken un kan den Kop dar ni dör krigen van sin langen Bart.

Then he wants to go there and can't get his head out of his long beard.

7.3

Do stekt he sin Bart darerst dör de Luk, un as he de darhendör het, do geit Fro Mansrot bi un schuft de Luk grad to mit 'n Bant, de se dar anbunnen het, un de Bart blift darin vast sitten.

So he sticks his beard through the hatch for the time being, and as he is standing there, Mrs. Mansrot goes over and shoves the hatch straight up with a bit she has tied to it, and the beard sits in it.

7.4

Do fangt he so jammerlik an to kriten, dat deit üm so sär:

Then he begins to complain that it's like this:

7.5

un do bidd't he är, se mag üm wedder loslaten.

and then he asks her to let go again.

7.6

Do segt se er nich as, bet he är de Ledder deit, war he mit to'n Barg herut sticht.

Then he doesn't tell her until he's been stabbed in the leather.

7.7

Do mag he willen oder nich, he mot är seggen, war de Ledder is.

Whether he wants to or not, he has to tell her who the leather is.

7.8

7.9 Do bint se 'n ganzen langen Bant dar an de Schuf un do legt se de Ledder an un sticht to 'n Barg herut, un as se baven is, do lukt se de Schuf apen.

Then she puts on the leather and stabs it into the bar, and when she is finished, she lets go of the leather.

7.10 Do geit se na när Vader hen un vertelt, wo dat är all gan is.

Then she goes to the father and tells him where she has gone.

7.11 Do freut de König sick so un är Brögam is dar ok noch,

The king is so happy and his brother is still there,

7.12 un do gat se hen un gravt den Barg up un finnt den ollen Rinkrank mit all sin Golt ün Sülver darin.

and then she goes up and digs the bar and finds the old rinkrank with all his gold in it.

7.13 Do let de König den ollen Rinkrank dot maken,

Then the king lets the old rinkrank die,

7.14 un all sin Sülver un Golt nimt he mit.

and he takes all his silver and gold with him.

7.15 Do kricht de Königsdochter den ollen Brögam noch ton Mann un se lävt recht vergnögt un herrlich un in Freuden.

Then the king's daughter gives the old man a husband and they laugh happily and joyfully.

Die Krystallkugel

The Crystalline Ball

1.1 Es war einmal eine Zauberin, die hatte drei Söhne,
die sich brüderlich liebten, aber die Alte traute ihnen
nicht und dachte, sie wollten ihr ihre Macht rauben.

Once upon a time there was a sorceress who had three sons
who loved each other as brothers, but the old woman did
not trust them and thought they wanted to rob her of her
power.

1.2 Da verwandelte sie den ältesten in einen Adler,

So she turned the eldest into an eagle,

1.3 der mußte auf einem Felsengebirge hausen und man
sah ihn manchmal am Himmel in großen Kreisen auf
- und niederschweben.

who had to live on a rocky mountain and was sometimes
seen soaring up and down in the sky in great circles.

1.4 Den zweiten verwandelte sie in einen Walfisch,
der lebte im tiefen Meer und man sah nur, wie er
zuweilen einen mächtigen Wasserstrahl in die Höhe
warf.

She transformed the second into a whale, which lived in
the deep sea and was only seen occasionally throwing up a
mighty jet of water.

Beide hatten nur zwei Stunden jeden Tag ihre
menschliche Gestalt.

1.5

Both only had their human form for two hours a day.

Der dritte Sohn, da er fürchtete, sie möchte ihn auch
in ein reißendes Tier verwandeln, in einen Bären
oder einen Wolf, so ging er heimlich fort.

1.6

The third son, fearing that she would also turn him into a
ferocious animal, a bear or a wolf, went away secretly.

Er hatte aber gehört, daß auf dem Schlosse der
goldenen Sonne eine verwünschte Königstochter
säße, die auf Erlösung harrte;

1.7

But he had heard that in the castle of the golden sun
there was a cursed king's daughter, who was waiting for
redemption;

es müßte aber jeder sein Leben daran wagen,
schon dreiundzwanzig Jünglinge wären eines
jämmerlichen Todes gestorben und nur noch einer
übrig, dann dürfte keiner mehr kommen.

1.8

but every one would have to risk his life for it, twenty-three
youths had already died a miserable death, and only one
was left, and then no one else would be allowed to come.

Und da sein Herz ohne Furcht war, so faßte er den
Entschluß, das Schloß von der goldenen Sonne
aufzusuchen.

1.9

And as his heart was without fear, he made up his mind to
go to the castle of the golden sun.

Er war schon lange Zeit herumgezogen und hatte es
nicht finden können, da geriet er in einen großen
Wald und wußte nicht, wo der Ausgang war.

1.10

He had been wandering about for a long time and had not
been able to find it, when he came to a large forest and did
not know where the exit was.

1.11 Auf einmal erblickte er in der Ferne zwei Riesen, die winkten ihm mit der Hand, und als er zu ihnen kam, sprachen sie:

Suddenly he saw two giants in the distance, who beckoned to him with their hands, and when he came to them, they said,

1.12 »Wir streiten um einen Hut, wem er zugehören soll, und da wir beide gleich stark sind, so kann keiner den anderen überwältigen;

"We are fighting over a hat, to whom it shall belong, and as we are both equally strong, neither can overpower the other;

1.13 die kleinen Menschen sind klüger als wir,

the little people are cleverer than we are,

1.14 daher wollen wir dir die Entscheidung überlassen.«

so we will leave the decision to you."

1.15 »Wie könnt ihr euch um einen alten Hut streiten?«

"How can you quarrel over an old hat?"

1.16 sagte der Jüngling.

said the youth.

1.17 »Du weißt nicht, was er für Eigenschaften hat, es ist ein Wünschhut;

"You don't know what properties it has, it's a wishing hat;

1.18 wer den aufsetzt,

if you put it on,

1.19 der kann sich hinwünschen wohin er will und im Augenblick ist er dort.«

you can wish wherever you want and at the moment it's there."

»Gebt mir den Hut.« sagte der Jüngling,   1.20
"Give me the hat." said the young man,

»ich will ein Stück Weges gehen und wenn ich euch   1.21
dann rufe, so lauft um die Wette, und wer am ersten
bei mir ist, dem soll er gehören.«
"I will go a little way, and when I call you, run for it, and
whoever gets to me first shall have it."

Er setzte den Hut auf und ging fort, dachte aber an   1.22
die Königstochter, vergaß die Riesen und ging immer
weiter.
He put on his hat and went away, but thought of the king's
daughter, forgot the giants and went on and on.

Einmal seufzte er aus Herzensgrund und rief: »Ach,   1.23
Once he sighed from the bottom of his heart and cried,
"Oh,

wäre ich doch auf dem Schloß der goldenen Sonne!«   1.24
if only I were in the castle of the golden sun!"

Und kaum waren die Worte über seine Lippen, so   1.25
stand er auf einem hohen Berge vor dem Thor des
Schlosses.
And no sooner had the words passed his lips than he was
standing on a high mountain in front of the castle gate.

Er trat hinein und ging durch alle Zimmer, bis er in   2.1
dem letzten die Königstochter fand;
He entered and went through all the rooms until he found
the king's daughter in the last one;

aber wie erschrak er, als er sie anblickte: 2.2
but how startled he was when he looked at her:

294

2.3 sie hatte ein aschgraues Gesicht voll Runzeln,

she had an ashen face full of wrinkles,

2.4 trübe Augen und rote Haare.

dull eyes and red hair.

2.5 »Seid Ihr die Königstochter, deren Schönheit alle Welt rühmt?«

"Are you the king's daughter whose beauty all the world praises?"

2.6 rief er aus. »Ach.« erwiderte sie,

he exclaimed. "Ah." she replied,

2.7 »das ist meine Gestalt nicht, die Augen der Menschen können mich nur in dieser Häßlichkeit erblicken, aber damit du weißt wie ich aussehe, so schau in den Spiegel, der läßt sich nicht irre machen, der zeigt dir mein Bild, wie es in Wahrheit ist.«

"that is not my form, the eyes of men can only see me in this ugliness, but so that you know what I look like, look in the mirror, it cannot be deceived, it shows you my image as it really is."

2.8 Sie gab ihm den Spiegel in die Hand und er sah darin das Abbild der schönsten Jungfrau, die auf der Welt war, und sah, wie ihr vor Traurigkeit die Thränen über die Wangen rollten.

She gave him the mirror, and he saw in it the image of the most beautiful maiden in the world, and saw the tears of sadness rolling down her cheeks.

2.9 Da sprach er: »Wie kannst du erlöst werden?

Then he said, "How can you be saved?

2.10 Ich scheue keine Gefahr.« Sie sprach:

I shun no danger." She said,

»Wer die krystallne Kugel erlangt und hält sie dem   2.11
Zauberer vor, der bricht damit seine Macht und ich
kehre in meine wahre Gestalt zurück.
"Whoever obtains the crystalline orb and holds it up to the
sorcerer will break his power and I will return to my true
form.

Ach.« setzte sie hinzu,   2.12
Alas." she added,

»schon so mancher ist darum in seinen Tod gegangen,   2.13
und du, junges Blut, du jammerst mich, wenn du dich
in die großen Gefährlichkeiten beziehst.«
"many a man has gone to his death because of it, and you,
young blood, you make me wretch when you involve
yourself in great dangers."

»Mich kann nichts abhalten.« sprach er,   2.14
"Nothing can stop me." he said,

»aber sage mir, was ich thun muß.«   2.15
"but tell me what I must do."

»Du sollst alles wissen.« sprach die Königstochter,   2.16
"You shall know everything." said the king's daughter,

»wenn du den Berg, auf dem das Schloß steht,   2.17
hinabgehst, so wird unten an einer Quelle ein wilder
Auerochs stehen, mit dem mußt du kämpfen.
"if you go down the mountain on which the castle stands,
there will be a wild aurochs at a spring below, with whom
you must fight.

2.18 Und wenn es dir glückt, ihn zu töten, so wird sich aus ihm ein feuriger Vogel erheben, der trägt in seinem Leibe ein glühendes Ei, und in dem Ei steckt als Dotter die Krystallkugel.

And if you succeed in killing him, a fiery bird will rise from him, carrying a glowing egg in its womb, and in the egg is the crystalline ball as a yolk.

2.19 Er läßt aber das Ei nicht fallen, bis er dazu gedrängt wird, fällt es aber auf die Erde, so zündet es und verbrennt alles in seiner Nähe, und das Ei selbst zerschmilzt und mit ihm die krystallne Kugel, und all deine Mühe ist vergeblich gewesen.«

But he will not let the egg fall until he is forced to do so, but if it falls to the ground, it will ignite and burn everything in its vicinity, and the egg itself will melt and with it the crystalline sphere, and all your efforts will have been in vain."

3.1 Der Jüngling stieg hinab zu der Quelle,

The young man descended to the spring,

3.2 wo der Auerochse schnaubte und ihn anbrüllte.

where the aurochs snorted and roared at him.

3.3 Nach langem Kampfe stieß er ihm sein Schwert in den Leib und er sank nieder.

After a long fight, he plunged his sword into its body and it fell to the ground.

Augenblicklich erhob sich aus ihm der Feuervogel   3.4
und wollte fortfliegen, aber der Adler, der Bruder
des Jünglings, der zwischen den Wolken daherzog,
stürzte auf ihn herab, jagte ihn nach dem Meer hin
und stieß ihn mit seinem Schnabel an, sodaß er in der
Bedrängnis das Ei fallen ließ.

Immediately the firebird rose from him and wanted to fly
away, but the eagle, the young man's brother, who was
flying among the clouds, swooped down on him, chased
him towards the sea and struck him with his beak, so that
he dropped the egg in his distress.

Es fiel aber nicht in das Meer, sondern auf eine   3.5
Fischerhütte, die am Ufer stand, und die fing gleich
an zu rauchen und wollte in Flammen aufgehen.

It did not fall into the sea, however, but on a fisherman's
hut that stood on the shore, which immediately began to
smoke and was about to burst into flames.

Da erhoben sich im Meere haushohe Wellen,   3.6

Then waves as high as houses rose up in the sea,

strömten über die Hütte und bezwangen das Feuer.   3.7

flowed over the hut and overcame the fire.

Der andere Bruder, der Walfisch, war   3.8
herangeschwommen und hatte das Wasser in die
Höhe getrieben.

The other brother, the whale, had swum up and raised the
water.

Als der Brand gelöscht war,   3.9

When the fire was extinguished,

suchte der Jüngling nach dem Ei und fand es   3.10
glücklicherweise:

the young man searched for the egg and fortunately
found it:

3.11 **es war noch nicht geschmolzen,**

it had not yet melted,

3.12 **aber die Schale war von der plötzlichen Abkühlung durch das kalte Wasser zerbröckelt und er konnte die Krystallkugel unversehrt herausnehmen.**

but the shell had crumbled from the sudden cooling by the cold water and he was able to take out the crystal ball unharmed.

4.1 **Als der Jüngling zu dem Zauberer ging und sie ihm vorhielt,**

When the young man went to the magician and held it up to him,

4.2 **so sagte dieser:**

he said:

4.3 **»Meine Macht ist zerstört und du bist von nun an der König vom Schloß der goldenen Sonne.**

"My power is destroyed and from now on you are the king of the castle of the golden sun.

4.4 **Auch deinen Brüdern kannst du die menschliche Gestalt damit zurückgeben.«**

You can also use it to give your brothers back their human form."

4.5 **Da eilte der Jüngling zu der Königstochter, und als er in ihr Zimmer trat, so stand sie da in vollem Glanz ihrer Schönheit und beide wechselten voll Freude ihre Ringe miteinander.**

Then the youth hastened to the king's daughter, and when he entered her room, she stood there in the full splendor of her beauty, and they both exchanged rings with each other with great joy.

Der goldene Schlüssel

The Golden Key

1.1 Zur Winterszeit, als einmal ein tiefer Schnee lag, mußte ein armer Junge hinausgehen und Holz auf einem Schlitten holen.

One winter, when the snow was deep, a poor boy had to go out and fetch wood on a sledge.

1.2 Wie er es nun zusammengesucht und aufgeladen hatte, wollte er, weil er so erfroren war, noch nicht nach Hause gehen, sondern erst Feuer anmachen und sich ein bißchen wärmen.

When he had gathered it up and loaded it, he did not want to go home yet, because he was so frozen, but first wanted to light a fire and warm himself a little.

1.3 Da scharrte er den Schnee weg, und wie er so den Erdboden aufräumte, fand er einen kleinen goldenen Schlüssel.

So he scraped away the snow, and as he was clearing the ground, he found a small golden key.

Nun glaubte er, wo der Schlüssel wäre, müßte auch das Schloß dazu sein, grub in der Erde und fand ein eisernes Kästchen.   1.4

Now he thought that where the key was, there must also be the lock to it, so he dug in the ground and found an iron box.

»Wenn der Schlüssel nur paßt!« dachte er,   1.5

"If only the key fits!" he thought,

»es sind gewiß kostbare Sachen in dem Kästchen.«   1.6

"there are certainly precious things in the box."

Er suchte, aber es war kein Schlüsselloch da, endlich entdeckte er eins, aber so klein, daß man es kaum sehen konnte.   1.7

He searched, but there was no keyhole; at last he discovered one, but it was so small that you could hardly see it.

Er probierte und der Schlüssel paßte glücklich.   1.8

He tried it and the key fitted happily.

Da drehte er einmal herum, und nun müssen wir warten, bis er vollends aufgeschlossen und den Deckel aufgemacht hat, dann werden wir erfahren, was für wunderbare Sachen in dem Kästchen lagen.   1.9

Then he turned it once, and now we have to wait until he has unlocked it completely and opened the lid, then we will find out what wonderful things were in the box.

Möwenstein Books

www.mowenstein.com

Renowned Authors

H. G. Wells · Ernest Hemingway
H. P. Lovecraft · Lewis Carroll
Franz Kafka · Friedrich Nietzsche
Albert Einstein · Oscar Wilde
Hans Christian Andersen

Notable Works

Frankenstein · Alice in Wonderland
Heart of Darkness · The Great Gatsby
Siddhartha · The Metamorphosis
Thus Spoke Zarathustra

Translation Services

We offer translation services in various languages, including German, Spanish, Chinese, Korean, Arabic, and more. For custom translations or revisions, please contact us at:

Email: translation@mowenstein.com

Our Collections

Franz Kafka Collection

- The Metamorphosis / Die Verwandlung
- The Trial / Der Prozess
- The Castle / Das Schloss
- and many more...

Pakt mit dem Teufel

- Faust Parts I & II by Johann Wolfgang von Goethe
- Doctor Faustus by Christopher Marlowe

Portraits of Irishmen

- The Picture of Dorian Gray by Oscar Wilde
- A Portrait of the Artist as a Young Man by James Joyce

Children's Classics

- Winnie-the-Pooh / Pu der Bär
- Brothers Grimm Fairy Tales
- Fairy Tales Told for Children
    - Author: Hans Christian Andersen

Visit Us

At Möwenstein Books, we are committed to providing high-quality bilingual editions of classic works. Explore our collections and discover more titles across various genres and languages.

Website: www.mowenstein.com